Healthy Habits Suck

How To Get Off The Couch & Live A Healthy Life ... Even If You Don't Want To

Dayna Lee-Baggley, PhD

16pt

Read How You Want

LARGE PRINT BOOKS, BRAILLE & DAISY

Copyright Page from the Original Book

Publisher's Note

Book printed in the United States of America

Distributed in Canada by Raincoast Books

Copyright © 2019 by Dayna Lee-Baggley
New Harbinger Publications, Inc.
5674 Shattuck Avenue
Oakland, CA 94609
www.newharbinger.com

Cover design by Sara Christian

Acquired by Elizabeth Hollis-Hansen

Edited by James Lainsbury

Library of Congress Cataloging-in-Publication Data on file

TABLE OF CONTENTS

"*Healthy Habits Suck* is the right companion on a journey toward eating, sleeping, and living well. This book is solidly grounded in research and years of practical experience bringing a refreshing 'what works' attitude. You will find accessible activities, compelling descriptions, and profoundly relatable insights into living a healthier life. If you're struggling to make healthy lifestyle changes, try this radically new approach to living well."

—**Timothy Gordon, MSW, RSW,** award-winning coauthor of *The ACT Approach* and *Mindful Yoga-Based Acceptance and Commitment Therapy*

"So many of us fail again and again to keep up the healthy eating or exercise goals we set for ourselves. In this readable, realistic, and honest book, Lee-Baggley combines cutting-edge behavioral science, professional (and personal) experience, and usable techniques to show us how we can make the changes that matter to us, and make them stick. I think this book will help many of my clients: I KNOW it will help me!"

—**Ray Owen, DClinPsychol,** consultant clinical and health psychologist (National Health Service, England), and author of *Living with the Enemy*

"*Healthy Habits Suck* is a breath of fresh air and a much-needed compassionate perspective on the difficulties of making lifestyle changes. Lee-Baggley writes with the perfect blend of easy-to-understand science, illustrative clinical examples, and personal experience to help the reader change their perspective on what it means to be healthy, and the best ways to pursue health goals."

—**Jason Lillis, PhD,** coauthor of *The Diet Trap,* and assistant professor at the Brown University Medical School

"The central premise of this book is that most health behaviors go against our natural instincts (apple pie will always taste better than apples). So, how do you get yourself to do them? Here, Lee-Baggley provides a key insight: rather than linking health behaviors to specific goals like 'losing weight,' sustained change happens when we link these behaviors to a deeply felt value like 'maintaining my independence.' The book is an easy read, with real-life case studies and strategies on how to approach decision points and engage in mindfulness and self-compassion. A good read for anyone seeking to change their behaviors."

—**Arya M. Sharma, MD,** professor of medicine at the University of Alberta, Edmonton; and founder of Obesity Canada

"Healthy Habits Suck is a laugh-out-loud introduction to the passengers on your bus who hijack your efforts to pursue healthy habits. How do we live with our caveman brain's instincts in the modern world? Lee-Baggley has a goal: to help you live a more meaningful, purposeful, and vibrant life through emotion-focused coping strategies to manage your health behaviors—even when you don't want to."

—**Denise Campbell-Scherer, MD, PhD,** professor in the department of family medicine, and associate dean of the lifelong learning and physician learning program at the University of Alberta, Edmonton

"This is one of the most useful and important books I have read for some time. The skills you will learn from this book are based on the latest theories and research in the fields of psychology, health, and behavior change. The book will be especially useful to anyone interested in becoming more active, eating better, (re)engaging with a hobby, or improving their health in other ways. But I would also recommend this book if you'd like to become clearer about your personal values, or if you want to learn how to find more meaning and purpose in your daily life."

—**Paul Flaxman, PhD,** reader in the department of psychology at City, University of London; and coauthor of *The Mindful and Effective Employee*

"Lee-Baggley helps us appreciate our very human affinity for adopting and practicing poor health habits, year after year. Then, she provides practical strategies for humans to use to choose behaviors that promote health, one moment at a time. This little book helped me take on a small, important, and difficult change in my life because I want to live and love and be of service to others as long as I can. Thank you, Dayna Lee-Baggley, for sharing your stories and your wisdom with us!"

—Patricia Robinson, PhD, coauthor of *The Mindfulness and Acceptance Workbook for Depression*

To all my clients who have given me the honor of sharing their journey with me. Your resiliency inspires me every day.

Foreword

Why is it so incredibly difficult to be healthy?

Why do so many people struggle to initiate healthy behaviors that they know will make them happy?

Why do most common-sense approaches to health and wellness usually fail in the long term?

And what can we do differently to help ourselves build the sorts of lives we can truly and deeply appreciate—including but not limited to being physically and emotionally healthy?

These are a few of the key questions that Dayna Lee-Baggley explores and answers within this book using a science-based approach called ACT (Acceptance and Commitment Therapy). The ACT model offers a powerful set of realistic, practical, and evidence-based strategies to help you develop the kinds of healthy habits and behaviors that are the foundation of a purposeful and fulfilling life—all while effectively handling the pain that inevitably goes with it.

Hang on a moment: did I just suggest that pain is inevitable? Yes, I sure did. The inconvenient truth is that life is both wonderful and terrible. If we live long enough, we will experience both happiness *and* heartbreak, success *and* failure, love *and* loss, bliss *and* despair, health *and* illness, joy *and* regret. These opposites are a package deal, just like no one gets a free ride or a smooth journey. The fact is, life is difficult, and it serves up pain and suffering for us all.

But hey—it's not all bad! Fortunately for us, the ACT model gives us a way forwards in the face of life's many hardships. Acceptance and Commitment Therapy gets its name because of a key theme: it teaches us how to reduce the impact and influence of painful thoughts and feelings (acceptance), while simultaneously taking action to build a life worth living (commitment). And in the pages that follow, Dayna Lee-Baggley will show you, step-by-step, how to do this in the realm of health behaviors. Where you go from there is ultimately up to you.

Enjoy the journey; you are in good hands.

—Russ Harris, author of *The Happiness Trap*

INTRODUCTION

Healthy Habits Suck

If you google "how to be healthy," you'll find a whole bunch of websites offering easy and fast tricks. But guess what? They lie. Being healthy is hard. It's so hard that most of us are not healthy. The majority of North Americans eat too much processed food, don't sleep enough, drink too much, and are overweight. In fact, if you are a "normal" weight, you're actually abnormal—that is, you're in the minority, because most of us now live with overweight or obesity.

If you're someone who gets up every morning and can't wait for your run, considers eating sweet potatoes a splurge, and sets aside thirty minutes every morning to meditate—this book isn't for you. It sounds like you're already living your healthiest life! If you're someone who thinks about getting up to go for a run but goes back to sleep, regrets last night's fast-food dinner, and can barely remember how you got to work, let alone take the time to be mindful, then this book is for you! While there aren't statistics for what percentage of the United States is composed of these different types of people, rest assured that if you're one of the ones who doesn't want to exercise, you are not alone. In fact, I argue that you're part of the majority. Together we're going to figure out how you can live your healthiest life, even when you don't feel like it.

I won't offer you false hope in this book. I won't try to convince you that healthy living is easy, or that there's a type of exercise that will make you want to get up early to do it, or that broccoli tastes as good as ice cream. What I will offer you is an understanding, based on science, of why long-term healthy habits are so hard to maintain. I will provide you with tools that will help you increase your willingness to do the hard work of being healthy.

Being Healthy Is Hard!

Many of us know what we *should* be doing to be healthy, so I'm not going to spend much time on these topics. Most of us already know that we should sleep more, eat more vegetables, stop smoking, and exercise more often. If you have a health condition, it's likely there are a number of health behaviors you are supposed to do, such as restricting certain foods (for example, sweets) or engaging in more physical activity. There are also things that some of us think we should be doing to be healthy, such as yoga or walking in nature more often. In this book I'll use the term "health behaviors" to describe all these things, what we should be doing (or think we should be doing) to be healthy.

However, it's pretty clear that across the globe we're not doing the things we should be doing to be healthy. Diabetes among adults rose from 4.7 percent in 1980 to 8.5 percent in 2014 (World Health Organization 2018a). The obesity rate has more than tripled since 1975 (World Health Organization 2018b). More than one-third (36.5 percent, or 118.3 million) of US adults now live with obesity (Centers for Disease Control and Prevention 2018), and globally more than 1.9 billion adults live with overweight or obesity as of 2016 (World Health Organization 2018b). About 85.6 million Americans have some form of cardiovascular disease or suffer from the aftereffects of stroke (American Heart Association 2014). Nine in ten Canadians over the age of twenty have at least one risk factor for heart disease, and four in ten have three or more risk factors (Heart Research Institute 2018). On a broad scale, humans are not living a healthy lifestyle.

Being Healthy Is Abnormal!

So, if we all know we should be doing things to be healthy, why aren't we doing them? In my opinion, it's because health behaviors are abnormal. Yah, I just said that. It's probably shocking to hear such a thing, especially in a book about being healthy, but it's true. Almost every health behavior requires us to do something that goes against our natural instincts as humans.

Let's look at physical activity as an example. Imagine human beings millions of years ago, in the age of cave people. One caveman thought to himself, *I should go running.* His thoughts and feelings supported this plan: *Good idea! Let's do it!* So he got up early and went for a run. Another caveman thought the same thing, but his thoughts and feelings didn't support the idea: *Why bother? You can do it tomorrow. Besides, it's too cold out there.* So he laid back down in the cave and went back to sleep.

Later that day while hunting in the forest, a bear started chasing both cavemen. Who do you think ended up being lunch? If you picked the caveman who chose to sleep instead of going for a run, you are correct. (Keep in mind that just to survive they were both getting the amount of exercise that triathletes get nowadays, so they were both really fit to begin with.) He had more energy available when he needed it. As a caveman you didn't need to be the fastest, you just had to be faster than the other guy.

Now let's return to modern times. Let's say you're lying on your couch and you think, *I should go for a walk. My physician says I need to exercise more.* What happens? If you're a well-functioning human, the instinctive, automatic response is to *not* go for a walk but to rest. This is no accident. As a result of millions of years of evolutionary pressure, our automatic, natural instincts are to rest when we can. This behavior helped us survive as a species. Perhaps you felt too tired to get up off the couch or you thought *I can do it later.* This is exactly how your brain and body have evolved to work!

The same is true of how our brain and body react to fatty, sugary, salty foods. Parts of our brains "light up" when we eat them, the same ones that are activated by cocaine. (In fact, your brain lights up even more for sugar than it does for cocaine). What does this mean? It means that fatty, sugary, and salty foods were incredibly rewarding to cave people—and, by evolutionary extension, us—on a physiological level.

Millions of years of evolution have shaped humans to avoid pain, seek pleasure, take the path of least resistance, and live for today. These principles make complete sense when you consider the lives of our ancient ancestors. Pain was associated with life-threatening events or death; survival required a lot of energy, so they consumed foods with fat and sugar and conserved energy whenever possible by following the path of least resistance; and they focused on the here and now compared to what might be good ten years from now, because ten years from now didn't matter if you couldn't stay alive today (plus, their life span was only about thirty years). Cave people who followed these principles were more likely to survive an attack or a long winter without food and therefore had more offspring. So, over time, these behaviors shaped humans. And as we evolved, these behaviors turned into instincts hardwired in the human brain and passed down to future generations. This is why parts of our brain still respond as if we're living in cave people times. This is part of the reason why living healthy can be challenging.

Health behaviors require you to do the opposite of these principles: you have to experience pain and discomfort (for example, go for a run), avoid pleasure (for example, don't eat ice cream), take the most difficult path (for example, take the stairs instead of the elevator), and live for the future (for example, stop smoking because it could kill you twenty years from now). It's worth repeating that health behaviors are abnormal!

Don't lose hope just because your instinctive responses aren't the healthy ones. You don't have to follow them. Every day we override our automatic instincts. Have you ever wanted to punch your boss because he was being super annoying, but you didn't—that's you overriding your instincts. If you got out of a nice warm bed this morning to go to work—that's you overriding your instincts. If you put money in a bank—that's you overriding your instincts. How do we do this? Our frontal lobe. In contrast to the ancient parts of our brain, the frontal lobe evolved more recently. It manages executive functions, such as delaying gratification and making plans. It can override all kinds of messages sent from the more ancient brain, but doing so requires deliberate effort. In this book you're going to learn how to harness your ability to override your instincts in order to live a healthier life.

About This Book

This book is partly based on my work, which has a foundation of field-tested science and, in particular, acceptance and commitment therapy. Acceptance and commitment therapy is a type of cognitive behavioral therapy that involves aspects of behavior change, mindfulness, and acceptance to address mental and physical problems. Literally hundreds of studies have examined the effectiveness of acceptance and commitment therapy for reducing human suffering by treating physical and emotional problems. I'm a researcher and a registered clinical psychologist who specializes in helping people with chronic health problems. Every day I encourage individuals to be healthier or teach health care providers how to encourage their patients to be healthier, so in this book I included many of my real-life experiences working with hundreds of people trying to improve their health. Some of these people had life-threatening health conditions, and some of them just wanted to look better in a bathing suit. In order to protect their confidentiality, I changed their names and aspects of their stories. In some cases I combined different parts of different stories, or I changed details.

This book is also about my personal experience. I am a generally healthy person who, until recently, didn't have to dedicate too much attention to being healthy. It's a running joke in my family that I hate vegetables (apparently going back to infancy), and I don't consider myself an athlete. For most of my life I was in a normal weight category, except when I was pregnant. Then, about two years before I wrote this book, my marriage ended. We did not have a "conscious uncoupling." Although

I felt the change would be a positive one in the long run, it was incredibly stressful and painful in the short run, and during this period I gained forty pounds. I tried to lose some of the weight with minor corrections that had been successful in the past, but nothing seemed to work. At one point I was exercising six days a week, including going to boot camp three times a week, running "hills" twice a week, running a 10K every Sunday, and watching my diet. With all that effort I lost nothing. Zilch. Zero. In fact, I continued to gain weight! Perhaps you're thinking, as I did—briefly—that I was gaining muscle. Wrong! Expensive body-fat testing indicated that I was not losing fat.

It was eye-opening to realize I was experiencing what so many of my clients had described: that their efforts to be healthy, lose weight, or control blood sugar had no effect. It was humbling to have to provide obesity-management treatment to individuals and groups when I myself was forty pounds overweight. I felt like a fraud, and I found myself needing a reason to continue being healthy when it seemed to have no effect on my weight. I began using all of the techniques and tools I'd been providing clients for years. I had to "walk the walk" so I could continue to stand in front of individuals and groups and encourage healthy living, even if my body didn't show it.

This is all to say that I didn't write this book as someone who has it all figured out. At the time of this writing, I still haven't lost all my "divorce weight," *and* I still continue to engage in healthy behaviors. As I have learned to say to myself: *I live as healthy as possible; what my body does with it is not up to me.* So, not only have many of the suggestions in this book been field-tested on clients, they've also been tested by me. As someone who would much rather lie on the couch and eat ice cream, I'm on this journey with you.

That's the broad abstract for the book. Here's an overview of the topics we'll explore:

Part 1: Being Healthy Is Hard

- Identifying values and how they can motivate us to do the hard work of being healthy (chapter 1)
- Recognizing what we do and don't control, and learning how to focus on what we do control (chapter 2)

Part 2: How to Be Healthy ... Even if You Don't Want To

- How to deal with thoughts and feelings that get in the way of engaging in health behaviors (chapters 3 and 4)
- How to use mindfulness and self-compassion skills to engage in health behaviors (chapters 5 and 6)

Part 3: Living a Healthy Life

- How other people impact our lives and how to deal with those who may help or hurt our health behaviors (chapter 7)

- How to handle relapses in health behaviors (chapter 8)
- How to integrate health behaviors in the long term (chapter 9)

Your Healthy Habit

In order to make working through this book as practical as possible, I suggest that you pick one healthy habit to focus on, such as going to the gym, eating more fruits and vegetables, or reducing sugar consumption. It should be a habit you haven't been able to successfully stick to. In each chapter you'll learn different skills to help you improve your chances of sticking with it. These skills build on each other, and by the end of the book you'll have a whole toolbox full of skills to help you live a healthier life.

In this book we'll be using an adaptation of the choice point model (Ciarrochi, Bailey, and Harris 2013) to help you stick with this healthy habit. This model outlines how with any challenging situation you can move *toward* or *away* from what matters to you. In this book, you're going to focus on moving toward your healthy habit. There will be things that get in the way of you engaging in this healthy habit, so you'll be learning a bunch of skills that will help you stick to it more often. The goal of this model is to help you give yourself a choice point, which is a conscious, deliberate choice to engage in a heathy habit and move toward what matters to you. Often we behave automatically, engaging in unhealthy habits without fully being aware of doing so. The goal of this worksheet and this book is to help you make more conscious choices for your health.

You can download a copy of the choice point worksheet at http://www.n ewharbinger.com/43317. You can write down the healthy habit you want to work on at the bottom. You can choose any healthy habit that is important to you. For example, you might write "exercise more" as the healthy habit you want to work on. At the end of each chapter I'll ask you to add to this worksheet what you learned in the chapter. By the end of the book, your copy of the worksheet will include all the skills you've learned that will help you engage in your healthy habit, as well as the things that can get in the way. I recommend reading one chapter a week and doing its exercises and practicing its skills during that week. Each chapter builds on the one before it, as do the skills. By the end of the book, you'll be better equipped to stick with your healthy habit because of all the choice points you'll be able to give yourself.

Choice Point

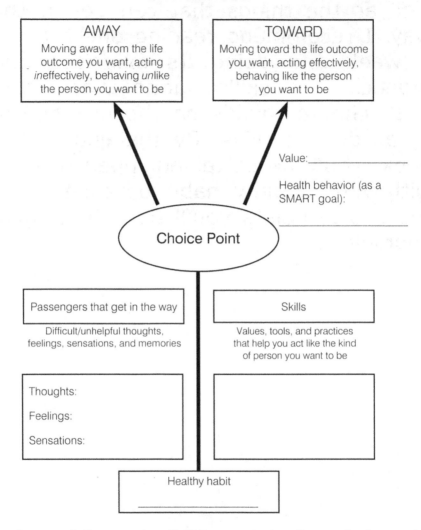

Adapted from the "Choice Point" worksheet in Ciarrocho, Bailey & Harris, 2013

Lastly, a host of online accessories (worksheets, exercises, and audio scripts) that augment the content of this book is available for download at http://www.newharbinger.com/43317. See the back of the book for details about accessing this material.

So, in this book I'm not going to try to make health behaviors easier, because I can't, but I am going to offer you skills to motivate yourself to be willing to undertake the difficult acts of being healthy—even when you don't want to.

PART 1

Being Healthy Is Hard

CHAPTER 1

The Marathon Runner Who Hated Running

In my efforts to lose my divorce weight, I decided to join a running club. One day I found myself running with a man who was turning seventy. He was a much better runner than me, and despite our age difference I had to keep asking him to slow down! While discussing the topic of running, he said to me, "Oh, I don't enjoy running." This came as quite a shock, considering he had already run more than a dozen marathons. He explained, "I don't actually enjoy the *act* of running. But I really enjoy *being a runner.*" He said he felt quite accomplished and proud when he told other people that he runs marathons. Thus, this man who had run more than a dozen marathons didn't like running, and yet he kept running because he had found something important and meaningful in the act.

Why on Earth Would You Engage in Health Behaviors?

Have you chosen a healthy habit to work on that you haven't successfully stuck with? Whatever you've chosen, I'm willing to bet it's something that goes against our human instincts. As I noted in the last chapter, millions of years of evolution have shaped humans to avoid pain, seek pleasure, take the path of least resistance, and live for today. Over time, these strategies became instincts that showed up automatically, and they were tremendously helpful for our early ancestors, as they still can be today. For example, if you accidentally put your hand on a hot stove, your instincts jump into action, and you take your hand away from the source of pain *without conscious awareness.* Your hand moves before you even register the pain. This is an ancient instinct at work.

Let's examine some typical healthy habits to see if they violate our instincts. Eating more vegetables? Yup, sure does: seeking pleasure. There are no receptors in your brain that respond to vegetables like they do for sugar. Going for a walk? It violates the instinct to take the path of least resistance. No matter how many times you go for a walk, it will *always* take more effort to walk than to lie on the couch. Training for a marathon? This completely violates the instinct to avoid pain. Avoiding junk food? Yes, indeed. This violates the instinct to live for today. Almost every health behavior goes against your natural instincts, and therefore health behaviors suck. They inherently don't feel good. So why on earth would you engage in health behaviors if they suck so much?

Values

Values are the qualities and characteristics that we would most like to express and represent in our lives; they are what matter most to us; they represent how we want to engage with the world. Values aren't just a thing, a noun, such as "parent." They include qualities, such as being adventurous, caring, creative, resilient, and persistent. A value is being an *engaged* parent, a *compassionate* spouse, an *artistic* worker. Values also have an emotional resonance: they just feel right. You don't have to explain why a value matters to you, you just know.

Western culture is very focused on goals, which are different from values. *Goals* are things that happen or don't happen. Once we achieve a goal, we usually stop pursuing it and move on to a new goal. For example, let's say you have the goal of losing weight, so you go on a diet. If you reach your goal weight, then what do you do? Many people stop doing whatever it is they were doing to lose weight. This is entirely consistent with the notion that when you achieve a goal, you move on to a new goal and stop working on the goal you just achieved. Do you see the problem? If you stop engaging in the health behaviors that resulted in weight loss, you're likely to regain the weight.

Unlike goals, values are more like a direction you head in. Imagine that heading west is an important value of yours. You might hit certain landmarks or cities along the way that will let you know you're headed west, but these markers (goals) alone aren't all that matters—every step heading west matters. Also, you'd never be able to "get west" in the goal sense. If heading west was a value, you'd always be trying to head in that direction.

Here's a less abstract example: if being a caring and loving person is a value of yours, then you have to continue to express that value all the time, such as by kissing your child or telling your husband you love him daily. You may hit markers along the way that let you know you're living this value, such as getting married, but you could never say, "Well, in 1985 I was super kind to my sister, so I'm good." Values don't work that way; you have to keep expressing them.

Let's briefly explore your values. I assume that you're reading this book because you want to be healthier, so answer this question for yourself: Why do you want to be healthier? Most people say they want to feel better, be more confident, have more energy and be more active, live longer, or avoid some bad health outcome (for example, diabetes, heart disease, cancer). Does your answer fall along these lines? The problem is we often don't go any deeper than this by asking, What am I going to do what that extra energy, confidence, health, and longevity? The way you answer this question helps reveal what really matters to you—your values (for example, traveling, exploring, dancing, playing music, and so forth).

I had such a discussion with a woman living with obesity who really wanted to stop eating her favorite snack, jelly beans, so she could lose weight. I started with the standard question: Why do you want to lose weight? And she gave the standard answer: "So I can be healthier." I probed further: Why do you want to be healthier? "So I can be more active." Why do you want to be more active? "So I can be healthier and lose weight." We went around in circles like this, yet I continued to press: What will you do with better health and extra energy? "I'll be able to walk stairs better. It hurts too much right now to do stairs." And what matters to you about being able to walk up stairs better? With this question, she suddenly burst into tears and said, "I have to move out of my family home because I can't walk up the stairs." Through her tears she explained, "This is my dream home. I've lived in it for forty years. I raised all my children there. I wanted to spend the rest of my life there ... but I can't because I can't handle the stairs anymore."

I was in tears at this point, too. That she had to give up something that meant so much to her because of her health was so poignant and painful. Just "wanting to be healthier" may not make giving up jelly beans worth the effort, but wanting to stay in her dream home just might be. (The "Clarify Your Values" exercise, available for download at this book's website, http://www.newharbing er.com/43317, can help you sort through your values.)

Linking Values and Health Behaviors

You've identified some of your values and the healthy habits you want to engage in. Let's work to link one of your values with one of your health behaviors. You can download the "Linking Values and Behaviors" worksheet at this book's website: http://www.newharbinger.com/43317. Remember, the goal is not to make "health" or "fitness" or "being active" a value. Real sustained change happens when we're able to link a health behavior to an existing, deeply felt value.

Ask yourself these questions:

How will engaging in the health behavior help me move toward a value?

How does engaging in the health behavior help me express a value?

Why does this health behavior matter? And what matters to me about that?

Here are some examples of ways to link a value and a health behavior:

- **Directly linked:** When I go for a walk I'm expressing my value of contact with nature.
- **Means to an end:** If I eat more vegetables, I am at a healthier weight, and if I'm at a healthier weight then I'm funnier and more sociable (value = humor/engaged relationships).
- **Think outside the box:** I value honesty. I need to track my food to be honest with myself about what I'm eating.

I follow a plant-based diet. It's similar to a vegan diet (no dairy, no meat) but focuses on what I do eat rather than what I don't eat. It's supposed to improve my health, but that's really just a bonus. The main reason I started this diet has to do with climate change. Reducing my contribution to this phenomenon is important to me. It turns out that the agricultural industry related to meat production typically contributes more greenhouse gases per person than does driving a car. That's to say that eating animal-based foods was probably generating more greenhouse gases than driving my car. For me, linking the value of "doing my part to reduce greenhouse gases" to this diet motivates me to stay on it, and the diet has the side effect of being a healthy choice for me.

Here's an example of how a client of mine linked behaviors and values. He came to see me to learn how to better manage diabetes. He knew he should be doing healthy things, but he never seemed to get around to them. Specifically, he wanted to get on the treadmill every morning (his health behavior). Here's the discussion we had:

Me: What about getting on the treadmill is important to you?

Client: My sugars are better. My day is generally better. I have more energy.

Me: Why is it important to you to have more energy?

Client: So I can do more things. So I can be more prepared.

Me: So when you have more energy you tend to be more prepared? And what is important to you about being more prepared?

Client: Things go more smoothly.

Me: What is important to you about things going more smoothly?

Client: People around me are happier. I get along better with my family. I can enjoy them more.

Me: And it matters to you to have good relationships with your family members?

Client: Yes, very much.

Me: So getting up in the morning is not just about managing your sugars. It's also about your values regarding getting to enjoy your family more.

Through this inquisitory process he and I were able to link his stated health behavior with values, and this connection allowed him to better stick to getting on the treadmill—even when he didn't want to.

Apple Pie Will Always Taste Better Than Apples

What tastes better, apple pie or apples? Uh, apple pie. You may eat a healthy diet such that the sugar and fat in apple pie is a shock to the system, and you may feel quite tired and yucky after eating apple pie, but your brain is *hardwired* to get excited about sugar and fat (apple pie) and not apples. What feels better, lying on the couch or going for a run? Lying on the couch! Again, your brain is hardwired to prefer the path of least resistance. It doesn't matter if you're a triathlete. You may get used to expending energy in a certain way, but it will *always* take more energy to go for a run than it does to lie on the couch.

All health behaviors have pros and cons. Pros include things like improved mood, more energy, or being able to stay active with grandkids. Cons include things like expending effort and being sweaty and uncomfortable. Research shows that when the pros outweigh the cons, you're more likely to engage in and stick with a health behavior (Hall and Rossi 2008).

There are different ways to make the pros outweigh the cons. One option is to make the pro side "heavier." Another option is to make the con side "lighter." People in your life (especially your health care providers) may try to make the con side lighter by trying to convince you that a health behavior isn't that bad ("After a while you won't notice the side effects of your medication" or "You'll get a runner's high and feel so good!"). I know many physiotherapists who recommend that their patients find an exercise they enjoy—that is, find an exercise with fewer cons to it. Well, many of us (including my marathon-runner friend) don't enjoy exercise. I have run a half marathon and more than a dozen 10Ks, and I have never had a runner's high. So I say that it's totally okay to hate every minute of exercise. You don't have to find an exercise you'll enjoy. Your exercise can continue to suck. We don't have to decrease the cons of the behavior in order to do it. Instead we can increase the pros.

You can dramatically increase the pros of a health behavior by linking it to your values—to what makes it worthwhile to you. In fact, research supports the benefit of this (Hall and Rossi 2008). The reasons for doing the behavior become more meaningful as a result and have a stronger pull. It's always going to take effort to exercise, so rather than trying to convince yourself that the health behavior won't be that bad, you should acknowledge how much the health behavior sucks and figure out *what will make it worth it for you.*

We Do Difficult Things All the Time

I was working with a woman who was having a hard time quitting drinking. Quitting was really important for her because she had a liver condition, and alcohol was very detrimental to her health. We talked about why she wanted to be healthy. She said she wanted to have more energy (a typical response). "What will do you with that extra energy," I asked.

She said she would use it to clean up her house, to do her dishes and her laundry. I stared at her. "You mean we're doing all of this work just so you can do more laundry? Well no wonder you don't want to quit drinking. I wouldn't quit drinking either if it meant I was going to have to do more laundry."

With further digging we identified that the reason she wanted to clean her house was so she could socialize more by having people over. Being more social and having friends over? Now that's likely to motivate someone to give up drinking. Ask yourself, How will engaging in these health behaviors help me be the person I want to be? What will make it worth it to do these health behaviors? Remember, health behaviors are hard! You need a really good reason to do them. If all you're going to do with improved health and extra energy is sit on the couch or do more laundry, then don't bother!

Here's another thing to remember: *We do difficult things all the time in the service of our values.* For example, if you got yourself out of a warm, cozy bed to go to work today, you did something difficult in the service of something that matters to you. Perhaps it's the paycheck, or perhaps it's the work that you do, but something motivated you to do something uncomfortable. If it matters to you to be an engaged, attentive, caring parent, then you do difficult things for your children in the service of this value all the time, whether it's cleaning up after your sick kid or staying up all night with a crying infant. It's totally okay if health isn't one of your core values. It's totally okay if engaging in a health behavior sucks. Engaging in your health behaviors can be just one more difficult thing you do in the service of your values.

Choice Point

You can download the choice point worksheet at this book's website: http://www.newharbinger.com/43317. At the top are boxes titled "toward" and "away." In the model, these represent whether a behavior moves you toward or away from the person you want to be or the life you want to have. In this chapter you clarified your values, which help you engage in behaviors that move you toward the person you want to be or the life you want to live. Go ahead and fill in the "value" line in the box under "toward." (I'll clarify what a SMART goal is in chapter 3, so for now just focus on your value.) "Strong" is a value that's important to me, so I'd write that on the "value" line.

If you're following my suggestion of reading one chapter per week, then this week try to focus on reminding yourself of your values and how the healthy habit you're working on is related to them. Thus, if you think about your healthy habit (for example, getting more sleep), try to also remind yourself of how engaging in it helps you be the person you want to be (for example, getting more sleep will help me be more creative, be a more engaged parent, and be more productive in my career or volunteer work).

CHAPTER 2

Weight and Other Things You Don't Control

I want to offer you a challenge: Tomorrow I'd like you to weigh 256 pounds; the day after that, 145 pounds; and the following day, 200 pounds. Do you think you can do this? Can *anyone* do this?

What if I asked you to drink one liter of water tomorrow, eat one cup of green veggies the next day, and go for a ten-minute walk the day after. Would you be able to do that?

Most individuals answer no to the first challenge but yes to the second. What's the difference between the two requests? The difference is how much control we actually have.

I'm going to say something that flies in the face of everything you know or have been told about weight: *We don't control our weight.* That's right, I just said that.

This may seem hard to believe. You've likely heard from the media, health care providers, and others in your life that if you just work hard enough, if you try for long enough, you'll be able to have a beautiful skinny body. Culturally we believe that we can control our weight, and that more effort results in more weight loss. There is a strongly held myth that weight is all about calories in and calories out, which led to a ridiculously simplified public campaign of "eat less and move more" (Chaput et al. 2014), but science actually tells us the opposite. We can *influence* our weight, but we don't have *direct control.* Here are just a few of the factors that influence weight (Hafekost et al. 2013; Schmidt et al. 2014):

- Genetics
- Maternal weight
- Paternal weight
- Maternal weight gain during pregnancy
- Whether you were breastfed

- Hormone levels, including cortisol, ghrelin, and leptin
- Sleep
- The walkability of your city
- Access to fresh fruits and vegetables
- The number of fast-food restaurants in your neighborhood
- The kind of job you have (for example, sedentary versus active)

With so many factors influencing weight, and the fact that we have very little control over most of them, it's impossible for us to have direct control over our weight.

The American and Canadian Medical Associations recently defined obesity as a chronic disease, which has several important implications. First, it means that the medical community will start to see and treat obesity not as a failure of character but a chronic condition similar to diabetes or high blood pressure. The second is that weight, similar to other chronic conditions, must be managed for the long term. Doctors would never treat someone's diabetes for only six months and then be confused why five years later the patient's blood sugar was out of control. Yet that's exactly how weight is approached. We expect that dieting for six months will have effects far into the future.

At the obesity clinic where I worked, participants often asked what the five-year outcomes were for our one-year program. We responded that obesity is a chronic condition that must be managed indefinitely. Our goal was to encourage participants to continue with their weight-related health behaviors for the long term.

As we've come to understand obesity as a chronic condition, and not as a failure of willpower, we've learned that we have a lot less control over our weight than we thought. In fact, not only does our culture trick us into thinking we have direct control over our weight, so does our own mind.

Our Problem-Solving Brain

Remember our cave person brain? One of the most critical things early humans had to do to survive was to problem solve, such as determining if they had enough water and food, and where they could find shelter. The problem-solving aspect of our brain comes in handy when we're trying to control aspects of the external environment, because these problems can be "fixed." If you need shelter, you can solve that problem. Food and water? Solvable! Thank you problem-solving brain!

However, this same problem-solving brain can also get us into trouble. Many of us in the developed world don't need to invest considerable amounts of effort in finding food or water or shelter. Most of the ways we solve these problems are straightforward and clear: go to the grocery store, turn on the tap, turn on the air conditioner. As a result of this relative ease, our problem-solving brain looks for other "problems" to solve, because it's hardwired to do this.

One of the other "problems" our brains will try to solve is weight, or any other chronic condition (for example, diabetes, chronic pain, heart disease). Our problem-solving brain identifies weight as a problem and works to get us to solve it or to get rid of it.

Western culture fuels our problem-solving brain with messages that weight is under our control, and if you're overweight you're a failure or you're lazy. Corporations capitalize on our tendency to want to fix things by pointing out what's wrong with us and by offering solutions to make us happy, and we buy these "fixes" by the boatload: weight loss was a 64-billion-dollar industry in 2014 (Marketdata LLC 2017).

One of my clients, Claire, was a classic example of someone who experienced negative consequences as a result of the problem-solving brain. Claire described to me the numerous diets, gyms, trainers, and weight-loss programs she'd used to try to lose weight. Like many people she had spent thousands of dollars, invested a huge amount of time and effort, and sacrificed things she enjoyed to "fix" her weight only to end up heavier than when she had started. Sound familiar?

A key issue with the problem-solving brain is that it tends to focus on the number on the scale as the goal and measure of weight-loss success. But using this number alone can actually lead to some unintended consequences in the long run. For example, Claire described adding exercise to her weight-loss efforts. "Every time I exercise I gain weight," she told me. Because losing weight was her goal, her understandable, natural response was to stop exercising because it wasn't helping. However, we know from research that exercise is important for long-term weight maintenance. Exercise also makes you healthier, regardless of your weight. But because exercise didn't result in short-term weight loss, Claire came to a natural, logical conclusion: Why continue to exercise if it's not helping me reach my goal? She therefore stopped engaging in that health behavior.

But even if you do lose weight, focusing on "fixing" your weight still has unintended consequences. Evelyn, another client of mine, successfully lost forty pounds by carefully counting calories, avoiding all social activities involving food, and knitting in the evenings (instead of eating chips while watching TV). When she finally got to her target weight, she was delighted (in fact, she celebrated by having her favorite food, an ice cream sundae). Being a well-socialized human in Western culture, once she reached her goal she stopped working on it and moved on to the next one. She therefore stopped doing all the behaviors that helped her lose weight. Not only did this make sense based on our understanding of goals (after all, she had accomplished her goal), but the behaviors she was engaged in to lose weight weren't sustainable over time. How was she going to avoid social activities involving food forever just to manage her weight? Science tells us that continuing with weight-related health behaviors long term is key to managing weight. As expected, when Evelyn stopped engaging in her behaviors she started putting the weight back on.

The inherent problem with a fix-it approach is that we focus on "getting rid" of the problem. By focusing on the number on the scale we assume that there is an "end" to the problem. When you fix it you're done. It therefore offers short-term solutions that don't result in long-term behavior change. Claire gave up because she never found the fix, and Evelyn gave up because she reached her goal and thought she was done. In both cases (whether you're succeeding or failing at losing weight), focusing on the number on the scale does not promote long-term behavior change.

Why do we need long-term behavior change? If you've struggled with weight then you have probably thought about and worked on your weight a great deal, sometimes even more than people who have been a "normal" weight their whole life. You've probably lost more weight in your life than these people. In fact, results from scientific research and my own clinical experience working with hundreds of people trying to lose weight clearly demonstrate this: weight loss isn't the hardest part of weight management—keeping the weight off, or weight maintenance, is (Chaput et al. 2014; MacLean et al. 2011). Just like any chronic disease, weight must be managed long term, not fixed with short-term solutions (Coughlin et al.

2016). The key to weight maintenance is continuing to engage in weight-related health behaviors over the long run. You therefore need a way to continue with health behaviors even when the scale doesn't change. How on earth do you do that?

After my divorce, I personally spent a lot of time *not* losing weight, and I had to figure out how to keep engaging in weight-related health behaviors even when they didn't result in weight loss. I mentioned that I follow a plant-based diet, not for weight loss but to reduce my environmental impact. I also go to boot camp three times per week. Again, I don't do this to lose weight, but to feel strong. Being able to do squats and push-ups and burpees makes me feel capable of tackling problems. While I was going through my divorce, feeling strong and capable was really meaningful for me. Even if I felt like an emotional wreck, I could still do some push-ups and remind myself that I could deal with whatever issue I was facing.

But despite this focus, my mind never stopped trying to get me to focus on weight rather than behavior. After all, a well-functioning mind is hardwired to relentlessly focus on fixing a problem. I had to remind myself that my job is to do my health behaviors; what my body does with that effort is out of my control. I had to repeatedly remind myself that my health behaviors were things I did in the service of my values (climate change, being strong and capable) rather than a "fix" for my weight.

Why Weight Isn't Fixable

If you've been socialized in Western culture, the belief that weight is fixable is typical. So I'm going to provide some more information about why weight isn't fixable. Over millions of years of evolutionary pressure human beings have evolved to make sure they don't starve death. For example, research shows that our metabolism slows down when we lose weight, a phenomenon referred to as "metabolic adaptation" (Muller and Bosy-Westphal 2013; Rosenbaum and Leibel 2010). Moreover, metabolism does not necessarily recover when weight is regained. For example, researchers followed the winners of the show *The Biggest Loser* for six years (Fothergill et al. 2016). After six years, contestants had regained 85 percent of their weight, but their resting metabolism was still at the slower rate it had been at after they'd lost weight. What does this mean? Let's take the average contestant.

At the beginning of the show, Mr. Average Contestant weighed roughly 330 pounds and could consume 2,600 calories and stay the same weight. At the end of the show he'd lost 130 pounds (he now weighed 200 pounds) and his metabolic rate had slowed. He could now only consume 2,000 calories a day and stay the same weight. After six years, he had regained 90 pounds (he now weighed 290 pounds) but his metabolic rate remained slow. He could only consume 1,900 calories a day and stay the same weight even though he had regained 85 percent of his original weight. So if you've lost weight and you feel like you're gaining weight just breathing air, you might be right.

But our bodies don't just stop at reducing our metabolism to make sure we don't starve to death (Tremblay et al. 2013; Dulloo, Jacquet, and Girardier 1996). Research shows that food will actually smell better one year after you lose weight. Food will also taste better a year after you lose weight. Why on earth would your body torture you like this? Well, it thinks it's just been through a famine, or a long, terrible winter with no food. Your body is desperate to put the weight back on to make sure you don't starve to death. You know all those skinny girls in the advertisements—they're not the ones who could survive a long, hard winter. Individuals who could put on extra pounds whenever food was available are the ones who survived—they are our ancestors.

Not only does your body encourage you to eat, it motivates you to eat all the things that are so-called unhealthy. Why are we motivated to eat "unhealthy" food? Consider the honey seekers of New Guinea. Members of this tribe climb about forty feet up a tree in order to reach into a beehive while dangling precariously in the air and getting stung. Sugar is so scarce in those parts that it's worth it. Let that sink in for a minute: this is the world our body and brain were adapted for, one in which sugar, fat, and salt are rare. Would you want to climb forty meters in the air and get stung by bees just to get a handful of sugar? Of course not! So your body developed a highly motivating system to make doing so worth it: the reward system of the brain.

This reward system releases neurotransmitters (chemicals in your brain) that make you feel awesome in order to motivate you to get sugary foods (McGonigal 2013). Interestingly, this reward system doesn't release these chemicals when you ingest the sugar, but rather in anticipation of ingesting the sugar. Have you ever anticipated that next bite of delicious food only to take the bite and not feel satisfied? This is the reward system in action! From the standpoint of survival, it makes no sense to be rewarded once you've gotten the food. If that were the case, you'd stop after ingesting the food. No, your brain is much smarter than that, because it wants you to survive! When we ingest the food, we don't feel satisfied, so we continue to want more until there's no food left.

What this means is that bodies that gain weight are doing exactly what they evolved to do. Despite everything you've been told, gaining weight is a natural consequence of a highly adaptive evolutionary system. If you are overweight, your systems are working exactly as they were intended to work. You're just not meant to live in an environment where you can ingest your total daily caloric needs in a single meal. I'm not saying that being overweight is healthy, but being overweight in our modern, Western world where food is so readily available is a natural, adaptive process—a consequence of millions of years of evolution.

So perhaps you're thinking, *Why haven't we evolved past this yet!?* Great question. The most important reason is that as you read this right now, there are humans somewhere on the planet starving to death. Starvation is still a threat to human life today.

What Do You Control?

At this point you might be feeling demoralized. Perhaps you're thinking, *Does this mean I'm going to be overweight forever? Does this mean there's nothing I can do about my weight?* There are things you can do. Just keep reading.

Let's try an experiment (inspired by Harris 2009). Recall how you bought this book. Maybe you ordered it online or maybe you went to a bookstore to buy it. And now completely forget how you bought this book.

Could you do it? Not likely. Deleting a specific memory or thought is not a typical human ability. Now let's try another experiment. Make your leg go completely numb. Remove any sensation or feeling from your leg, to the point that you could cut it off with a chain saw and not feel any pain.

Could you do that? Not likely. Okay, one more experiment: stand up.

Which one of these experiments was the easiest to do? Most people will say the final one. Compared to thoughts and feelings, we have far more control over our behavior. What do I mean by "behavior"? Behavior is something someone else can see you do, like standing up. If there was a reality TV show all about you, behavior is what we'd see you do on the screen. Behavior is not how you *feel* about your action, or whether you *wanted* to or *felt* motivated to do it, it's the action itself. The fact that we have control over behavior is great news! You can control health behavior—including going to the gym, walking, drinking water, consuming more fruits and vegetables, and integrating them into your life will make you healthier (and perhaps have the side effect of causing you to lose weight). In the next chapter we'll go over several exercises to help clarify health behaviors.

Health Behaviors Are the Goal

Changing your goal from the weight itself to health behaviors you engage in serves several purposes. First, you've created a goal you can actually control. If you work harder at trying to eat green veggies, you will likely eat more green veggies, whereas working harder to lose weight can sometimes have the opposite effect. Fixating on weight can lead to stress, which releases the stress hormone cortisol, and cortisol can interfere with weight loss (Jackson, Kirschbaum, and Steptoe 2017). From an evolutionary point of view, it makes sense that cortisol might prevent weight loss. Our mind interprets high levels of cortisol as being indicative of some type of danger. In cave person times, this might have been something like living through a long winter or a war. Cave people's bodies responded by conserving energy and storing fat so they'd have the resources to make it through the stressful event. Nowadays, though, stress isn't always linked to a need to put on weight. So the stress (and resulting cortisol) associated with the pressure one might feel to lose weight can actually prevent weight loss.

Here's a striking example. You might think that I lost weight when I trained for a half marathon. This was my assumption too. After all, I was running close to thirty kilometers a week. But I was gaining weight, not losing it. My trainer was not surprised. He said that running for more than an hour at a time decreases your metabolism and therefore can lead to weight gain. This makes sense from an evolutionary perspective. My body thought I must be under stress or facing a threat because I was spending a lot of energy running around! So, my body worked to conserve energy so I could keep running.

Second, focusing on behavior instead of weight creates a goal that is healthy. Focusing on health behaviors means you will end up healthier, regardless of whether you lose weight or not. This is important, because there is strong evidence that weight alone is not a good indicator of overall health. For example, consider body mass index (BMI), a method used by health care providers to qualify weight based on height and weight—in other words, it's another way of measuring weight. Health care providers often use this method to categorize an individual as "underweight," "normal," "overweight," or "obese," but BMI doesn't distinguish between a six-foot-two person who's 260 pounds of fat or 260 pounds of pure muscle. These two people both have a BMI of 33.4 and fall into the "obese" category. In fact, the BMI system categorizes many elite athletes as obese even though by all other methods they are considered extremely healthy. Some research suggests that if you don't have health complications, then you shouldn't be diagnosed as overweight or obese at all, regardless of what your BMI indicates. This research suggests that "obesity" is only a condition when excess adipose (that is, fat tissue) causes health complications (Sharma 2017). If you don't have complications, then you should just be described as having excess adipose but not as obese.

(Personally, I like saying "extra fleshiness.")

Additionally, research has shown that a single session of exercise can result in "healthier" fat cells (Van Pelt, Guth, and Horowitz 2017). Specifically, after exercise the fat cells had a greater ability for blood flow and to reduce inflammation, both of which are related to better overall health regardless of weight. Thus, even if you don't lose weight, you can be healthier at the weight you're at by focusing on health behaviors.

Third, changing your goal provides a reason to engage in health behaviors over the long term, and long-term behavior change is really the key to good health. Another study of *The Biggest Loser* contestants showed that those who continued to exercise after their time on the program were the ones most likely to keep the weight off (Kerns et al. 2017). This is a consistent finding in the literature: continuing to engage in health behaviors is associated with weight maintenance (McGuire et al. 1999). For example, the National Weight Control Registry (http://www.n

wcr.ws) is a research study currently tracking more than ten thousand people who have successfully lost weight (at least thirty pounds) and kept it off for at least one year. Studies using this database have repeatedly shown that participants who continue to engage in weight-related health behaviors, such as exercising, following a low-calorie diet, or watching less TV, successfully maintain weight loss in the long run.

Values

So if keeping up weight-related health behaviors is the key, how do we do it? By linking health behaviors with values. Managing your weight in the long run is going to suck. All weight-related health behaviors violate our basic principles of human functioning. So why on earth would you do them? Because engaging in your health behaviors may help you be the person you want to be.

Here's an example of what I mean. While discussing health behaviors with a woman living with obesity, she said she wanted to start eating more green vegetables. I asked her what eating more green vegetables meant for her. She replied, "It means I'm on a diet and I'm being punished because I've messed up again and gained weight." Well, if eating green vegetables represented "punishment" to her, no wonder she was struggling to eat more of them. Then we talked about why she wanted to lose weight in the first place. She offered the usual round of answers: to be healthier, to be more active, to live longer. But I kept digging deeper: What was she going to do with her improved health, extra energy, and extra years of life? Eventually she got around to the fact that she wanted to be healthier so she could continue to live independently. She didn't want to have to go to a home or be cared for by others. "I'm very stubborn" she reported. "I like to do things on my own."

"So it sounds like being stubborn and being independent are really important to you," I suggested. She agreed. "So, eating green vegetables is actually your way of being defiant. It's your way of telling the world to f*ck off because you're not going to a home. It's your way of being stubborn and independent."

Her eyes opened wide as she stared at me. "I never thought about it like that." And all of a sudden she was excited to go home and eat her green vegetables so she could tell the world to f*ck off.

If you flipped to this chapter hoping that I'd give you the magic key to weight loss, go back to chapter 1 and learn about the real secret weapon in life: living a values-based life.

Choice Point

In this chapter I discussed how we don't control our weight. This also applies to a number of other health outcomes, such as blood pressure, blood sugar, and cholesterol, and many of the goals we set for ourselves, such as "sleep more" or "be healthy." Our aim is to set a goal for ourselves that is achievable, a health behavior we can actually do, rather than something we don't control. For the choice point worksheet this week, consider whether your healthy habit is something under your control. Is your healthy habit an outcome or a behavior? Do you need to rethink your healthy habit? (See chapter 3 for more details on making your healthy habit a behavior.) My example of "exercise more" is a behavior and not an outcome. If I had instead listed "feel more energetic" or "be less tired" or "lose five pounds" as my healthy habit, then I would want to think about how I could recast them as health behaviors, because these are examples that are much less under my control.

PART 2

How to Be Healthy … Even if You Don't Want To

CHAPTER 3

Passengers on the Bus

In this chapter you're going to meet the passengers on your "bus" (adapted from Hayes, Strosahl, and Wilson 1999) and learn about the things that get in the way of health behaviors. Imagine you're a bus driver, and your passengers represent your thoughts and feelings and sensations. Some of the passengers are friendly and nice, but some are bossy and annoying. These passengers often like to tell us what to do. For example, imagine you're about to give a presentation at work. Your anxious passenger might say, "Oh no, what if you forget all your words? Maybe you shouldn't give the talk at all. You're just going to embarrass yourself." Or imagine you're about to get on a flight to go on vacation and you hear the announcement that the flight has been canceled and the next flight is two days from now. Your angry passenger might comment, "This is ridiculous! How can they do this? You better go give that airline employee a piece of your mind."

Sometimes it might feel like these passengers are driving the bus and taking us places we didn't mean to go. For example, every time I think *I should go to the gym,* there's a passenger on my bus who says, "You don't have time for that." Or if I think *I should pack my lunch instead of going out to eat,* this passenger says, "You don't have time for that." And sometimes I end up doing what the passenger says, telling myself, *Yeah, I have so much to do. I don't have time to go to the gym!* When this happens, the passenger is driving the bus, and I don't end up engaging in my health behaviors.

This is what passengers do; they take over the bus and knock us off our route when we're trying to engage in healthy habits. If we want to be a good bus driver and stick to our healthy habits "route," we need two main skills: to know the route we want to follow, and to be able to deal with passengers in a way that allows us to stick to our route. The good news is you've already done some work on determining your route. Your values are your route. In chapter 1 you clarified your values, or the direction you want to head in order to make a meaningful, vibrant, and healthy life for yourself and be the kind of person you want to be. But as you have probably experienced, knowing your values isn't enough to keep you on your route. Passengers are going to get in the way. So if you've ever had a thought or a feeling or a craving that stopped you from engaging in a healthy habit, this chapter is about learning skills to deal with your passengers so you can stick with healthy habits.

How Passengers Knock Us off Our Route

This is one of my favorite exercises (adapted from P. Flaxman, personal communication, February 23, 2016) for learning more about our passengers and how they knock us off our route. Stop for a moment and think about the healthy habit you've been working on with this book. When you think about having to accomplish this task and keep it up, what automatic reactions show up? What do the passengers have to say about the likelihood of you accomplishing this goal? Just pause and notice what thoughts and feelings show up. You can download the "How Passengers Knock Us off Our Route" worksheet at this book's website, http://www.newharbinger.com/43317, which will walk you through this exercise step-by-step.

Did any of your thoughts fall into any of the following categories?

☐ **Obstacles**

Our passengers point out all the obstacles and difficulties that lie in our path.

Example: *I won't have enough time.*

☐ Judgments

Our passengers tell us all the ways we're not up to the task.

Example: *I won't do it right.*

☐ Comparisons

Our passengers compare us unfavorably to others who seem to do it better, have more talent, or have it easier.

Example: *My sister can always do this. It's not hard for her.*

☐ Predictions

Our passengers predict failure, rejection, or other unpleasant outcomes.

Example: *You know you're never going to keep this up, so why bother?*

Did *most* of your thoughts fall into these categories? Congrats! You're a well-functioning human.

Remember our ancient cave person brain? Well, one very effective way to avoid pain and to take the path of least resistance is to avoid doing anything new. Cave person brains work on the principle that "The devil you do know is better than the devil you don't." That is, whatever your current circumstances, even if they suck, they're not killing you and are therefore safer than whatever unknown situation you might find yourself in if you tried something new. Your brain knows you can survive your current situation, but it doesn't know if you'll be able to survive some new situation. So the brain evolved to try to stop us from doing anything new, to make us cautious. Your brain isn't out to get you. It's genuinely (probably desperately) trying to keep you safe. It just doesn't know that this new or different thing you're trying to do isn't life-threatening in the modern world. So if you noticed your passengers giving you good reasons not to try something new, congrats! That's a sign of a well-functioning brain, but one that can also knock you off your route.

What to Do with Passengers...

Given that passengers can knock us off our route, how do we deal with interfering passengers on the bus? Perhaps you'd like to kick some of them off! Wouldn't that make sense? That's the most common response I get when I ask this question. "Wouldn't I be a lot healthier if I never had the thought *I don't have time for that?*" Of course! But have you ever found a way to *permanently* not feel angry or anxious? Have you found a way to not have certain thoughts? What I'm asking is, Have you ever been able to kick passengers off your bus permanently?

The answer is no, because the passengers on your bus, whether they're pain, anger, sadness, or any other kind of thought, are part of the human experience. Do you know anyone who doesn't experience pain or anger or sadness? (Remember, there's a difference between experiencing emotions and expressing emotions; I'm referring to experiencing emotions here.)

If so, that's not normal. Emotions are part of the human condition, and we can't get rid of them. We can't kick them off the bus. Sometimes you can take a detour to temporarily avoid passengers. For example, when I go to the land of wine and chocolate, I don't hear my passengers yelling at me quite as much, but this reprieve doesn't last long, and while on the detour I wasn't heading where I wanted to go. What else might you try, or have you tried? Let's look at a few possibilities.

Ignoring the passengers ... If kicking passengers off the bus won't work, maybe we can ignore them. That's a reasonable idea. But what do you think would happen if, in the real world, a passenger told the bus driver she wanted to get off at the next stop, and the bus driver completely ignored her? The passenger would likely get louder and more boisterous, maybe run to the front of the bus and yell, "I've got to get off the bus!"

Here's an exercise to get at what I'm talking about. Set a timer for thirty seconds. Then, for the next thirty seconds, please do not—I repeat, do not—think about pink elephants. Ready? Go.

(If you're like me, you probably skipped this exercise. I rarely actually do the exercises in self-help books. So if you decided to skip the exercise, I totally get it, but I invite you to reconsider. When I encounter an opportunity to try something new, one of my passengers says to me, "Oh, I know what that's about. I don't need to do it." Does this happen to you? But consider that it's impossible to learn a new skill without actually doing it. Right now is an opportunity to actually try something new. So I again invite you to try this brief exercise and perhaps notice what the passengers are telling you that might stop you from doing the exercise—that is, to try to knock you off your route.)

Okay, whether you did the exercise or not, perhaps you noticed that some of your passengers were trying to convince you to not do the exercise. Good job! Even if you didn't do the exercise but noticed your passengers, you're still actually doing something new!

If you did do the exercise, what did you notice? Most people report that they either thought about pink elephants or had to work really hard not to think about them. And just out of curiosity, have pink elephants been a big topic of conversation for you lately? Have you been texting a lot about pink elephants or chatting with coworkers about them? Is #pinkelephants trending on Twitter? Probably not. But having asked you not to think about pink elephants, you'll probably be thinking about them a lot more!

Why? Because of what's called the *thought suppression effect* (Wegner et al. 1987), which is a rebound effect. When you try to suppress or not think about a thought, you end up thinking about it more. The thought suppression effect makes it impossible to ignore your passengers. The more you try to ignore them while driving the bus, the louder and more insistent they'll get.

Negotiating with passengers ... Maybe we can negotiate with passengers. Have you ever had a debate in your head like this with a passenger: "Oh, look, your favorite:

cake! You should have some." *No, I can't. I'm trying to eat healthy.* "Yeah, but just this once. You can be healthy again tomorrow." *But I'm on a diet.* "Sure, but a little treat isn't going to hurt." I don't know about you, but I never seem to win these arguments. Not only do my passengers seem to be much better debaters than me, but they are offering much better options. I'm offering broccoli and they're offering cake; I'm offering going to the gym and they're offering lying on the couch. Basically the passengers offer behaviors consistent with our cave person principles, and I'm offering something that violates those principles. And while I'm debating them, all my attention is focused on them instead of sticking to my route.

Here's an exercise (Monèstes and Villatte 2011) to help you look at this another way. Over and over again, say "I cannot lift my arm" while actually lifting your arm. (Pay attention to what your passengers say to dissuade you from doing this exercise. This is another opportunity to try to do something new and to notice how your passengers try to knock you off your route.) This exercise illustrates that it's possible to *do the opposite* of what your passengers are telling you to do. You didn't have to convince your passengers you could do it. You didn't have to repeat positive mantras to convince yourself, like *You got this! You can raise your arm.* No, you simply lifted your arm even while you were telling yourself not to. In other words: you don't have to win the debate with your passengers in order to stick to your route.

Here's another one to try. (Again, pay attention to what your passengers say to convince you to not do this exercise). Think *I'm too tired to lift up my arm* while lifting your arm. Can you do it? How about this one: *I'm too tired to go to the gym. I'm too tired to go to the gym.* Perhaps it's possible to go to the gym even when our passengers are telling us we can't.

What these exercises demonstrate is that we don't have to get consensus from our passengers to be able to stick to our healthy habits. You don't have to win the debate with the passengers. You can engage in healthy habits even when your passengers are saying the opposite. Think of it this way: The bus driver doesn't get on the bus and say, "Okay, I'm going to go up Main Street and then take a left on 5th and then a right on 6th Avenue. Is everyone okay with that?" No. He just follows his route, regardless of what the passengers say. Sometimes when I get caught up in the chatter of my passengers and need a bit of courage, I say to myself *I cannot lift my arm* while lifting it, just to remind myself that I don't need my passengers to agree. So, no, you don't need to convince your passengers to stick to your route. You can avoid the debate altogether.

Thanking passengers ... So if you can't ignore your passengers or negotiate with them, how can you deal with them in order to stay on your route? What do you think would happen if a passenger said this to a bus driver: "Hey, bus driver, we're very close to my house. Could you take the next left, and then the second right, and drop me off in front of the house with the red door?" Even the kindest bus driver will respond with some version of "Sorry, but I have a route to follow." This hypothetical interaction displays the type of relationship we want to cultivate with our own passengers. We want to acknowledge what they have to say but not let them divert us from our route. Remember, the passengers aren't trying to be mean, they're just working very hard to protect you. They just don't know that what you're trying to do is actually healthy for you. So, with some genuine gratitude, thank your passengers for sharing, and proceed along your route.

In the next section we're going to spend some time clarifying our healthy habit route and practicing ways to notice how our passengers try to knock us off our route.

Sticking to the Route: Committed Action

Some people think that the "acceptance" part of acceptance and commitment therapy (ACT) means that you don't do anything, but the therapy itself entails quite the opposite. The "commitment" part of ACT is all about changing behavior, which is referred to as committed action. We're going to more clearly define the healthy habit you're trying to cultivate so you can engage in committed actions. Take a moment to do the following exercise. You can write your answers in a journal, or you can download and use the "Do It Anyway: Committed Action" worksheet at this book's website: http://www.new harbinger.com/43317.

Step 1. Clarify Your Values

First, why are you working on this healthy habit? What is the deeply meaningful reason behind it? How is it linked to your values, to who you want to be in life?

Step 2. Make the Healthy Habit a SMART Goal

Once you've clarified or reminded yourself of the values this healthy habit can help you express, then you can set a SMART goal to help yourself achieve it. SMART goals are *s*pecific, *m*easurable, *a*chievable, *r*ealistic, and *t*ime bound. Here are some tools to help make sure your healthy habit is a SMART goal.

Is My Healthy Habit a Behavior? The first step in creating a SMART goal is to make sure your healthy habit is actually a behavioral goal, which will ensure that the goal is specific and measurable (the *S* and the *M* in a SMART goal). Many people will set motivational goals, such as "I will *want* to have a salad for lunch"; or emotional goals, such as "I will *enjoy* going to the gym"; or thinking goals, such as "I will stop *thinking* about food all the time"; or outcome goals, such as "I will *lose* fifteen pounds." The problem with such goals is that we have a lot less control over our motivation, feelings, thoughts, and outcomes than we do our behavior. A behavior is observable (other people can see you do it), measurable (something you can check off a checklist to document that it happened), under your direct control (not an outcome or something you can only influence), and meaningful (something that's related to your goals). Check to see if your healthy habit is a behavior that's observable, measurable, under your direct control, and meaningful to your goals. If not, ask yourself this: What would someone see me do if I was accomplishing my emotional (or behavioral, thinking, outcome) goal? Consider, for example, a motivational goal: "I will want to eat salad for lunch." If you were accomplishing this goal of "wanting" to eat more salad, what would someone see you do? Probably eat more salad for lunch. "Eating" the salad is a behavioral goal. "Wanting" to eat the salad is a motivational goal. Asking what someone would *see you do* will help you change the goal into a behavioral goal.

The "Do Instead" Goal: Remember the pink elephant exercise? It demonstrated how trying to not think about something usually results in one thinking about it more. Sadly, we do this all the time. What's the first thing people think about when they go on a diet? What they're *not* going to eat: *I'm not going to eat sugar, I'll stop eating junk food, I won't eat white bread.* Instead of creating a "don't do" goal, make a "do instead" goal.

One classic "don't do" goal for people at the obesity-management clinic where I worked was to stop eating in front of the TV late at night. Many clients described "doing so well" with their diet all day long only to have it all fall apart in the evening. There's a simple explanation why this is such a common experience. Willpower (or self-control, as psychologists like to call it) is what keeps us from doing the things we want to do but shouldn't, and it's like a muscle. We use this muscle all day long to get along with people and to do the things we need to do, so by the end of the day it's spent. Many people try to use their willpower to stop themselves from eating in front of the TV at the end of the day, but this is like asking an alcoholic to go to a bar and not drink. It's just a risky proposition.

Instead of setting yourself the goal to *not* eat in front of the TV, think of what you can do *instead* of eating while watching TV. Many people at the obesity clinic took up knitting, which is an incompatible behavior with eating—meaning you can't do both at the same time. I often suggest that clients donate their knitting to charities. In that way, knitting becomes a value-based action and isn't simply a distraction, further encouraging people to engage in it.

You could also figure out what you could do instead of ending up in front of the TV. Sometimes it's easier to avoid the TV altogether than to try to avoid eating while watching TV. A great "do instead" goal is to go to bed! Lots of research shows that getting more sleep is good for health (for example, Rod et al. 2014). There is increasing evidence that sleep plays an important role in weight loss and weight management (Cappuccio et al. 2008; Gangwisch et al. 2005; McNeil, Doucet, and Chaput 2013). In fact, when clients ask whether they should get up early to exercise or get more sleep, my colleague Dr. Sharma, an expert in obesity management (http://www.drsha rma.ca), says to get more sleep.

Take a look at the healthy habit you're trying to work on while reading this book. Is it a "don't do" or a "do instead" goal? If it's the former, can you change it? Instead of telling yourself to *not* think about pink elephants (or to not binge in front of the TV), think about what you're going to do instead.

The 90 Percent Rule: *Learned helplessness* is a psychological condition in which people feel they have no control over their environment, and that there's no way for them to win, so they give up even trying (Abramson, Seligman, and Teasdale 1978). When I conducted weight histories with clients at the obesity clinic, they would often tell me that they'd lost hundreds of pounds only to gain it all back, so they had given up. When we pick goals that are too big, or goals that we don't have any control over, we can induce learned helplessness. People only have to feel helpless a few times to create learned helplessness, but it takes nearly ten times as many experiences of having control to *undo* it. This is key: once learned helplessness has set in, we can continue to feel powerless even if our circumstances have changed and we now have some control. That's why it is really important to avoid continuous failure when setting a goal. That's where the 90 percent rule comes in.

Are you 90 percent sure you can accomplish your health goal within the time frame (the *T* in a SMART goal) you've set? If the answer is yes (you're 90 percent sure you can accomplish the goal), then proceed. If the answer is a weak yes or a maybe or a no, then rework the goal. Break it down into smaller, more manageable steps. For example, instead of walking five times a week for thirty minutes, try walking two times a week for thirty minutes or five times a week for ten minutes. Change the goal until you are 90 percent sure you can achieve it. If it's a 90 percent goal, you're ensuring it is achievable and realistic (the *A* and the *R* in a SMART goal).

Why is having a manageable goal important? Let's say you set the goal of walking five times a week for thirty minutes but only manage to go three times. Have you succeeded or failed? According to your goal you failed. On the other hand, let's say your goal was to walk two times a week for thirty minutes and you manage to go three times. You're a success! And we know that success breeds success. When we feel successful at something, we want to keep doing it.

Counting calories is an effective tool for managing weight, and my client Samantha was really struggling with it. Figuring out portion sizes was tedious and frustrating for her, and when she managed to record all her calories she often found that she'd gone over her calorie goal, which made her feel like a failure. She'd be really good tracking for a few days and then stop completely—that old learned helplessness. So we took a stab at applying the 90 percent rule: perhaps she could just record protein intake to try to get to a protein goal for the day, or only record breakfast because it was the easiest meal for her to record, or just record on Mondays, or set a calorie goal closer to what she was currently consuming so that even a small change in her diet would help her hit her calorie goal. She picked recording her calories on Mondays over a two-week period. Once she was consistently successful at that, I asked if she felt

90 percent sure she could record her calories on Mondays *and* Tuesdays? Through this process we added a series of 90 percent goals to get her closer to her overall goal.

You can string together a series of 90 percent goals (smaller goals) like this to reach your overall goal, a process known as shaping (Ramnero and Törneke 2008). While it might seem more time consuming to approach a goal this way, not succeeding won't get you any closer to your goal either. Success makes us want to try more often, whereas failure makes us want to give up and not try at all. Humans do not persist at things they know they can't achieve. This is just human nature.

So, if you're not 90 percent sure you can accomplish your goal in the time frame you set, then change the goal. Usually I recommend setting just one 90 percent goal at a time, or two at the most. If you try to do too many changes at once, even if each one is a 90 percent goal, you're probably not meeting the 90 percent rule overall.

That's why I asked you to pick just one healthy habit to work on with this book.

You may notice that your passengers have a lot to say about setting smaller (more achievable) goals: "You can't just record breakfasts, or food on Mondays, or protein! That doesn't count! You can't reach your goal this way!" or "You'll never get anywhere if you don't hit the *real* calorie goal." *Thank you very much, passengers.* Remember, they're not out to get you, but when you follow their advice you're not driving the bus where you want to go ... toward your healthy habit. So thank them for their advice and adjust your goal as necessary. Remember, research indicates that small and steady and successful progress will get you to your goal faster (Ramnero and Törneke 2008).

Putting It All Together: Here's an example, from my work, of creating a SMART goal with one of my clients who was going on vacation. She described how when she traveled she worked hard all day to stay on track with her diet, but in the evenings she binged on junk food. She was also a vegetarian and often found it difficult to find healthy vegetarian options while traveling. As a result she often ended up binge eating french fries and ice cream because "technically" they are vegetarian.

I shared with her an experience I'd recently had while traveling in Alberta. Before leaving for the trip, I had the sense that trying to maintain my plant-based diet was going to be problematic. Alberta is known for its AAA Alberta beef much more than for vegan or vegetarian food, so I came up with a SMART goal to manage my diet. I decided I'd order steak and vegetables for dinner and vegetarian no-cheese omelets for breakfast, creating a "do instead" goal while employing the 90 percent rule. Of course these meals completely violated my plant-based diet, but trying to stick to this diet on my trip wasn't a 90% goal. I felt these adjustments would help me manage calories so I didn't overdo it, and if I was going to eat meat, it might as well be high-quality meat. Keep in mind, I was making a conscious plan. This wasn't my passengers hijacking my bus. I made a deliberate choice to be as healthy as I could be in the context of my travel plans.

I pointed out to my client a few things about her goal: first, her goal, to avoid binge eating, was a "don't do" goal, and, second, it broke the 90 percent rule, because she felt certain she'd be "unable" to avoid the binge eating at night while traveling. So we came up with a "do instead" goal that she felt 90 percent confident she'd be able to adhere to during her weeklong trip: she would focus on increasing her vegetable and protein intake throughout the day, and at night she'd drink lots of water and not fight the urge to binge eat. She worked on accepting that the binge eating was likely to happen, because it was just too big of a challenge to address at the moment, so she'd focus on adding healthy things to her diet instead. No miracles occurred on her trip. She indeed binged every night, but she also managed to consume more vegetables, protein, and water, and because *that* had been her goal she felt successful. She also got to enjoy her trip more because she wasn't constantly dreading or trying to avoid binge eating in the evenings.

Rumble Strips

Okay, so you've set a SMART goal. Guess what? Those passengers are *still* going to have some commentary about your likelihood of succeeding. This is what happens when we try to do something new or different.

Imagine that your life is a highway (I'm pretty sure that's a song). If the current highway you're on, and where it's leading you, totally works for you, then keep going! If you're headed toward a life that matters to you, then stay in the lane. But if you're thinking *How did I get on this path,* or *This wasn't totally what I meant my life to be,* then you need to consider exiting the highway.

Where I live there are rumble strips on the side of the highway that are designed to alert drivers when they're veering off the road. They grab your attention—wake you up, for example, if you've dozed off. If you've ever hit a rumble strip you know they're loud, bumpy, and uncomfortable. There are no rumble strips at exits, which is nice, because who wants the shock of crossing one when all you want to do is leave the highway. But if you've decided you want to leave the metaphorical highway you're on, your passengers are going to put rumble strips in your way. They don't want you to take the exit and try something new; they want you to stick to what you know. This is your passengers trying to keep you safe. Remember, their motto is "The devil you do know is better than the devil you don't know." From your passengers' point of view, however yucky the current highway might be, it's better than the unknown. What kind of rumble strips are they going to place in your path? Maybe you'll feel anxious, or maybe you'll think *I can't do it* or *Why bother?* Whatever form they take, they're designed to be uncomfortable and alarming and to keep you on the same old path.

So how do you get off the highway in spite of this? There's no difference between hitting a rumble strip on purpose rather than accidentally. It's still bumpy, noisy, and uncomfortable—but it's not shocking, because you saw it coming. So if you're not headed toward a life that matters to you, if you're not becoming the person you want to be, then you may have to experience some discomfort in order to change—that is, accept the rumble strip of your passengers to find a different path. Changing course is not about waiting until doing so feels easy; it's about being *willing* to feel uncomfortable in the service of your values.

Behaviors Self-Assessment

The "Behaviors Self-Assessment," available for download at this book's website (http://www.newharbinger.com /43317), is a useful way to track how consistent you're being with your health behaviors, and, by extension, your values. If you're reading the book one chapter per week, then you can use this tool to track your practice of the new skill that we discuss in each chapter over the course of the week. Alternatively, you can use this tool on a daily basis or at whatever frequency makes sense for your SMART goal. For example, if my value is taking care of the planet and my healthy habit is following a plant-based diet, I can mark how consistently I've engaged in this behavior by placing a mark somewhere in the bull's-eye. When I was in Alberta, I was on the outside of the bull's-eye. When I returned home and was making my own meals, I was closer to the center. As you use this tool, notice if your passengers have any comments on the likelihood of you following through with the tracking. Remember ... *thank you passengers!*

Behaviors Self-Assessment

DATE:_____

| Value: |
| Health Behavior: |

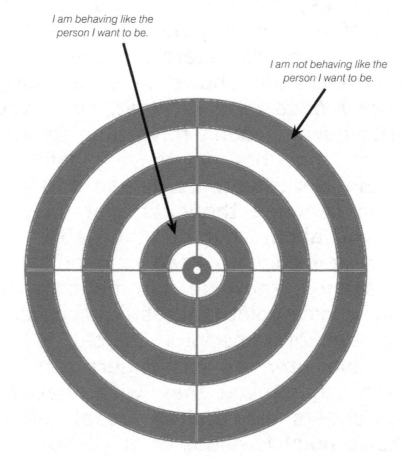

I am behaving like the person I want to be.

I am not behaving like the person I want to be.

Adapted from Dahl and Lundgren 2006

Choice Point

Let's take a look at the choice point worksheet again. You can now add the passengers (the difficult or unhelpful thoughts, feelings, sensations, and memories) that show up and get in the way of your healthy habit. For example, when I try to exercise, one of the passengers that shows up is the thought *I don't have time for that,* so I would write down "I don't have time for that" under "thoughts" on the left-hand side of the worksheet. Go ahead and write down common thoughts that show up for you about your healthy habit.

A key point to keep in mind is that passengers show up automatically, and your choice point (that is, your potential moment of conscious choice) is only possible *after* the passengers show up. Even though you may wish that your passengers didn't show up at all, the choice point is about what you do *after* they show up, and not about whether they show up or not. That is, I don't have a choice about whether I feel tired or whether I think *I don't have time for that.* These passengers show up automatically. But I do get to choose what I do *after* I notice these passengers. Our goal is to slow ourselves down enough when our passengers show up so we can choose to move toward or away from our values in a conscious, deliberate way. The aim is to be able to be more aware of our passengers and our values in order to create more choice points—more opportunities to make a choice to move toward our values. Try to create more conscious choice points by slowing down and noticing your passengers and reminding yourself of your values. Doing so can increase the likelihood that you move toward your healthy habits and your values.

In chapter 1 you added a value in the box under "toward" on the worksheet. In that same box you can now record your healthy habit as a SMART goal. Ask yourself if it's a "do instead" goal; if it passes the 90 percent rule; if it's specific, measurable, achievable, realistic, and time bound? If the answer to any of these questions is no, see how you might change the behavior so you can say yes to all the questions. My healthy habit of "exercise more" isn't a SMART goal. For example, it's not specific enough to be measurable. However, if I change the goal to "go to the gym for twenty minutes two times per week" (and I think I'm 90 percent sure I can do this), then I've created a SMART goal. It's specific and measurable (I'll know I did it if I went twice for twenty minutes). Because I'm 90 percent sure I can do it, it is achievable and realistic, and I know I'm going to try to do it within seven days, so it's time bound. See if you can do the same for your healthy habit, and record it on the worksheet.

CHAPTER 4

If You Don't Like the Weather, Wait Ten Minutes

The limbic system is an ancient part of our brain that contains a number of automatic processes concerned with survival, including our emotional reactions. Emotions often function as messengers that provide us with important information. Imagine that an emotion is like a delivery person who has a very important package to get to you, and he won't stop until it's delivered. Many of our emotions are designed to be uncomfortable because they're supposed to motivate us to do something, such as move away from a threat. Unfortunately, our modern world often presents us with perceived threats that we can't get away from; there's nothing we can "do," but we still get the emotional reactions. For example, have you ever been angry while sitting in traffic? Or worried about what the future might bring? Congratulations! You're a well-functioning human being.

If you've ever had a cookie or a drink of alcohol or a smoke to deal with a stressful day or a bad mood, then you know that emotions can play a major role in our ability to stick to our healthy habits. Emotion passengers often knock us off our route. In this chapter we're going to explore our emotion passengers and develop skills to deal with them so we're better able to stick to our healthy habits route.

Our Fix-It Brain

Remember our wonderful problem-solving brain? It has been a useful tool for humans in our evolution. Unfortunately it likes to work on fixing—or getting rid of—our feelings, which can get us into trouble. Take, for example, my client Anna. She came to me because she felt she was drinking too much. We quickly discovered that she was experiencing a lot of stress and anxiety. And in response to all this, she drank.

Although Anna felt that she was defective, that there was something wrong with her, her mind was actually working exactly how millions of years of evolution had shaped it to work. She noticed feeling anxious and then tried to do something to make herself feel better, which was to drink. This strategy for feeling better actually *did* make her feel better, but it only worked temporarily. Because she's a normal human, her anxiety came back. And then, on top of that, she was now mad at herself and criticizing herself for her behavior—for letting her emotion passengers reroute her bus. What we discussed was that the anxiety wasn't the problem, it was the "solution" she used to get rid of it. This is often the case.

We all end up doing things to avoid feeling bad, and many of our unhealthy habits feel awesome in the short term! They are very effective short term "fixes" for feeling bad. Are there things you do that help you get rid of a feeling in the short run but interfere with your healthy habits? Maybe it's eating chocolate after a stressful day.

Maybe it's snacking on treats when you're bored. Maybe it's drinking or smoking to relax. (You can write your answers on the "What Have You Done to Avoid Feeling Bad?" worksheet, available for download at this book's website: http://www.newharbinger.com /43317.) There's nothing dysfunctional about what you're doing. Humans are hardwired to avoid pain, and whatever you're doing works in the short run. It's in the long term that these strategies create problems, because they often divert us from our route and therefore don't help us build a healthy life that matters to us.

Just Don't Worry About It!

Not only has our mind been shaped to help us avoid bad feelings, we receive this message in all kinds of ways in Western culture. Loved ones, strangers, ads, the media—they all tell us that if we just tried hard enough, we'd be able to change our feelings, as if we can will ourselves to not feel sad or worried or mad.

Let's try a thought experiment to see if you can will yourself to not feel anxious (adapted from Hayes 2005). Imagine that you're in a dunk tank, and the lever that releases the seat you're sitting on is connected to electrodes taped to your body. If you experience anxiety, these electrodes relay the information to the lever, triggering it to drop you in the pool. In order to motivate you to not feel anxious, the pool is full of sharks. All you have to do to avoid falling into the pool of sharks is to *not* feel anxious. Could you do it? Could anyone do it? Probably not, despite the awesome motivation. And yet we're constantly told that we should be able to change our feelings.

We also constantly receive messages to ignore our feelings or to invalidate them. My eight-year-old son's school sent him home with a handout describing a few scenarios for which he needed to come up with a compassionate response. The first scenario was "Your sister falls down and hurts herself. She is crying. What can you do?" He wrote, "Tell her she's fine."

Noooooo! I thought. *That's not compassionate at all!* I was horrified!

But later that week at one of his hockey games, a kid fell down and the coaches started yelling, "You're fine! Get up! You're fine!" I realized that this was what he'd been taught to do when someone was hurt. You don't have to be at a sporting event to observe this type of behavior. Head over to a playground and wait for a child to fall down. Inevitably a parent will say, "You're fine." As parents we say things like this to our kids all the time. We don't intend to invalidate their feelings, quite the opposite. We're trying to make them feel better. But the result is we're teaching kids to ignore, change, or fix their feelings. When it doesn't seem okay to feel our feelings, we often engage in unhealthy habits to (temporarily) make the feelings go away. Let's explore another option.

Welcoming an Old (Smelly) Companion

Here's another thought experiment (inspired by Hayes, Strosahl, and Wilson

1999, and Oliver 2011). Imagine that you've decided to host a party and invite lots of people. You're having a great time, but soon your smelly, rude neighbor Brian comes in and starts bothering your friends. You kick him out and go back to the party, but while you're busy having a good time, he slips back in. You throw him out a second time, and this time you decide to stand at the door to make sure he doesn't get back in. This works, but while you're guarding the door you realize that you aren't enjoying the party. So you decide to go back to the party even though that means Brian will return. And before long he does, but rather than fight with him you decide to just let him be. He's still smelly and annoying, but you accept that in order to be able to enjoy the party, you have to accept him being there.

In this experiment, Brian is like our feelings. We do all kinds of things (that is, stand at the door) to avoid bad feelings, and often the cost of these efforts is that we don't get to enjoy life (that is, the party). The alternative is to accept our feelings in order to enjoy life. *Acceptance* doesn't mean you like something, want it, or even enjoy it; it's "taking what is given" (Harris 2008), acknowledging what is, and having a willingness to let it be as it is. Accepting your feelings involves making space for them so you don't have to fight with them as much. I'm not talking about *tolerating* feelings, I mean *welcoming* or *embracing* them. It's not just tolerating an acquaintance, it's welcoming a friend, a companion. The unhealthy habits we do to avoid our feelings are totally normal; however, if you allow yourself to just feel your feelings, as yucky as they may be, you wouldn't need unhealthy habits. In other words, you're accepting the message from the messenger but not letting the message take over or change your route.

Here's another way (inspired by Harris 2008) to think about accepting your emotions. Imagine two bordering countries that disagree on finances, religion, culture, language—pretty much everything. They have choices about how they deal with their differences. They could be at war with each other (fighting each other), they could have a truce (tolerating each other), or they could have a peace treaty (accepting each other). If they are at war, they have to dedicate a lot of resources to this fight and there will likely be casualties. If they have a truce, they would still need to keep up their military resources in case they need to go to war, and they would have to actively monitor the border to watch for signs of danger. If they have a peace treaty, they don't have to dedicate resources to fight or be prepared to fight. Instead they can dedicate their resources to important things such as education, health, arts, or productivity. The treaty does not, however, require that they like each other or agree to adopt the other's language or culture. By accepting your feelings, you're aiming to not just tolerate them (have a truce), but rather to welcome them (have a peace treaty). Imagine what you might be able to do with all the energy you've reclaimed by not fighting.

Here's an exercise to practice this idea of developing a peace treaty with your feelings (adapted from Lillis, Dahl, and Weineland 2014). You can write your answers on the "My Old Friend" worksheet, available for download at this book's website: http://www.newha rbinger.com/43317. Or you can record your answers in a journal or on a separate sheet of paper. Think about an emotion you don't like to experience, perhaps guilt, anger, sadness, or shame, and then answer these questions:

When do you first remember experiencing this emotion (or something similar to it)?

How old is this emotion?

Do you know anyone who has never experienced this emotion?

Where, when, and how has this emotion shown up in your life?

What have you done to try to avoid this emotion, change it, or make it go away?

Given all these efforts, have you succeeded in permanently ridding yourself of this emotion?

This emotion has been with you for a long time. Rather than fighting with it, could you welcome it like smelly old Brian?

Feelings Are Just Being Feelings

What happens if you take a puppy for a walk and you let the puppy be in charge? What happens to your walk? It's all over the place! You go smell the grass, you go backward to see a rock, you go look at a tree and pee on it. You're definitely not getting from place A to place B in a direct manner. In fact, you're likely to end up in some unintended places.

But should we blame the puppy? No. The puppy is just being a puppy. The problem is we're not being responsible pet owners. The same holds true for your feelings: anger is just being anger, shame is just being shame, sadness is just being sadness. Problems arise when we let our feelings be in charge of our direction (or take over our bus). Just like allowing a puppy to be in charge, we end up in unintended places when we let our feelings run the show. So, our job as responsible emotion owners is to be in charge of where we go. Gently and kindly bring your feelings with you while sticking to your route. Be very kind to your feelings, just as you would be to a puppy. Remember, you're not just trying to tolerate your feelings, you're welcoming them and treating them with the same kindness you would an unruly puppy.

What happens if you leave a puppy alone in your house all day? Disaster! But, again, the puppy was just being a puppy. The problem was that we left the puppy unattended and didn't check in on it. The same can happen with our feelings. When we don't check in and keep an eye on our feelings, they can get into trouble. But feelings are just being feelings. It's our job to keep an eye on them.

How can you keep an eye on your feelings? It involves periodically checking in with yourself to see what you're feeling. Pause and notice sensations in your body, such as tightness in your shoulders or a churning in your stomach. See if you can be curious about these sensations and feelings, and try to be kind to them when you notice them. Imagine holding and taking care of feelings the way you would a puppy.

And then return to what you were doing.

Many of us worry that as soon as we let feelings in, they'll overwhelm us. We may have been holding them back for so long that we're worried about a tsunami. By doing the exercise described above and checking in on your feelings, you can let them in a little at a time. There's a big difference between intentionally checking in on a feeling and having it spring up on you unexpectedly. Why don't you be in charge of your feelings instead of the other way around? (The worksheet "Check In on Your Feelings," available for download at this book's website (ht tp://www.newharbinger.com/43317, can help you practice checking in on your feelings.)

Here's another exercise to help you get in touch with what you're feeling without letting the feeling take over (inspired by Flaxman, Bond, and Livhelm 2013, and Harris 2009). A series of questions and an audio recording ("Feeling Object"), both available for download at this book's website (http:/

/www.newharbinger.com/43317), can help you with this exercise.

To start, imagine a stressful event or person in your life—not the most stressful thing, just something a little bit distressing. Aim for something that's about a 4 out of 10.

Think about this stressful event or person until you start to notice some feelings emerge. See if you can pay more attention to those feelings. Where do they show up in your body? What kind of sensations are there? Imagine drawing a circle around the place in your body where you feel them most intensely. Perhaps focus on the sensation or feeling you feel most intensely. Imagine being a curious scientist who has never witnessed it before. Examine it with some curiosity...

If this emotion is an object, what shape is it? How big is it? Is it heavy or light? What's it made of? Is it solid, gooey, or airy?

Imagine this "feeling object" pops out of you and is sitting on a table or the floor in front of you. Examine it with curiosity. Notice it in ways you've never noticed before. What's it like to see it outside of you in this way?

Now, welcome the feeling object back into your body where it belongs. Notice with curiosity any resistance or desire for it to stay outside of you, and then welcome the feeling object back inside of you *where it belongs...*

Now I invite you to imagine that with every breath you can make space for this feeling object inside you. Don't try to make it smaller or to make it go away, just give it more space so it's not bumping up against you quite as hard. Imagine that with every breath you expand the space around it, however you understand that to be...

What was it like to examine your feelings in this way, to interact with your feeling object, to make space for this feeling object without trying to make it go away in any way? Our goal with our feelings is not to make them go away but to make space for them. They are part of us, but they are not *us.*

You Are the Blue Sky

What if it was your job to make sure it was sunny and 80 degrees outside tomorrow. That would be a pretty stressful job, right? Well, feelings are similar to weather: we have about as much control over them as we do the weather. Sometimes you can *predict* how you're going to feel the same way we can generally predict the weather. For example, if you're a student heading into an exam, your mood may likely change for the worse. But we don't have direct control over our mood; we can't will ourselves to be happy or make ourselves not be worried (remember the shark-tank exercise?). Thinking about feelings the way we think about the weather can help us understand some key skills for managing our feelings.

I grew up in Calgary, Alberta, on the prairies of Canada. It was pretty dry in Calgary when I was growing up, only raining two to three times a year. My family of four owned only one umbrella, and that was plenty. Then I moved to Halifax, Nova Scotia, on the

Atlantic coast, where it rains a lot. One day while talking with a friend on the phone, she asked me what I was up to. I explained that I couldn't go outside because it was raining, and I was waiting for it to stop. She laughed. "If you won't leave the house when it's raining in Halifax, you'll never leave the house!" So I went out and bought rain pants, rain boots, and a raincoat—even a rain cover for my bag. So now when it rains, I can still go outside and live my life. So if we consider our emotions to be the weather, then continuing to live our life in spite of our emotions, such as being in a bad mood, is an important skill for managing our emotions. In other words, as I chose to not let the rain keep me from leaving my house, we don't let our emotions take over our day (or drive our bus).

In Canada we have snow days, when everything shuts down because of the weather. Sometimes the weather is so bad that you have to wait out the storm. Sometimes we have to do the same thing with our emotions. One of my close friends seems to live in "tornado alley" because she experiences a lot of wild moods and emotional meltdowns. When she's having an emotional storm, we go into the storm shelter together to wait it out. We hunker down and play cards, dominos, and board games and watch funny movies. She's still upset and periodically bursts into tears, but we just stick to waiting out the emotional storm. Sometimes we're scared of the weather, and sometimes we're worried about what will happen. This skill isn't about making the emotional storm enjoyable. It's about finding ways to wait the storm out because inevitably it will pass; inevitably our mood will change. You've probably heard the expression "If you don't like the weather, wait ten minutes." Like the weather, our moods are always changing.

If we consider our feelings to be like the weather, another important idea emerges. Sometimes our feelings seem overwhelming and overpowering. But if we think about our feelings as being *part* of us but not *all* that we are, then our feelings can feel more manageable. This idea is captured in this metaphor:

you are the blue sky; your feelings are the weather (inspired by Harris 2009). If your feelings are the weather, then you are the blue sky where weather happens. If that's the case, then your feelings are just things passing through your mind, as a tornado passes through the sky. You are not your feelings.

One of my clients, Anne, came to me for help to stop drinking. She and her husband had recently separated because she'd found out that he was cheating on her with a friend of theirs. She talked about how she felt angry all the time and that it was an overwhelming feeling. It had led her to do some things she wasn't proud of, including having screaming matches with her ex at her children's baseball games. So instead of causing scenes she had taken up drinking—too much. Considering her feelings to be like the weather and herself as the blue sky was a revelation for her: she was not her anger. It was a part of her but it was not her. She used a lot of the skills in this chapter to learn to make space for her anger so it didn't take over and lead her places she didn't mean to go, whether that was drinking too much or fighting with her ex.

If you are the blue sky and your feelings are the weather, then just as the worst hurricane or tornado can't damage the blue sky, and it eventually ends, your feelings can't damage you, and eventually they will pass. Sometimes we just have to wait out the storm. Does that mean it's fun to live through a tornado or a rainstorm? Of course not! Is it easier to live your life when it's sunny and 80 degrees compared to when it's rainy and stormy? Of course! But if I let the weather determine what I can get done, I'll forever be at the mercy of something I can't control. Our job is to make space for our feelings, to be the blue sky, so we don't have to engage in unhealthy habits to cope with our feelings and we can continue to do the things that matter to us.

How to Take Guilt for a Run

Guilt is an emotion that comes up often with my clients who are trying to engage in healthy habits. I frequently hear things like "Well, when I don't feel guilty, then I'll start going to the gym," or "Maybe when my daughter is older, I won't feel so guilty being away from her," or "I feel too selfish going to the gym when my family needs me." There's a good reason why guilt keeps showing up. Imagine what would have happened if, back in cave people times, all the parents abandoned the children to go do something for themselves? The tribe's survival would have been in trouble. Guilt showed up to make sure they did what was good for the tribe and not something selfish.

Think about that for a minute. Guilt had to motivate cave people to not take more than their share, or to be selfish, in a time when such behaviors—eating more food or drinking more water—were about simple survival. Well, no wonder guilt feels terrible! It's supposed to feel terrible. That's the tool the brain had available to get our ancestors to do something against their own well-being in order for the tribe to survive. This feeling works so effectively that it helped our species to thrive!

But in our modern world, selfishness may actually help the tribe. On Sunday mornings I have the option to go running with my running club or to watch my son play hockey. When I go running I feel proud of myself and I'm in a much better mood because I conversed with other friendly runners and I did something healthy for my body. All of this translates into me being a much better mom, a better member of my family (or "tribe"). If I go to the rink, I end up feeling resentful, tired, and stressed. So, rather than waiting for a day when I don't feel guilty about running, guilt and I go for a run every Sunday (okay, not *every* Sunday).

When I told this story in a workshop setting, the participants all started coming up with ways that I could make everyone feel better: "Maybe if you explain to your son..." and "Maybe if you go do other activities with your son..." and so on. This is what many of us do. We try to find ways to make everyone feel better before we act, but ... No! It sucks. He feels disappointed and I feel guilty, but I know I'm serving the greater good of my tribe. You might be wondering, How can you do this? It comes down to my willingness to feel discomfort in the service of my values. I remind myself that running isn't about losing weight or being selfish, it's about being a more engaged mom.

So if you feel guilty about doing something to take care of yourself or to engage in a healthy habit—congrats! You're a well-functioning human. Does this healthy habit move you toward or away from the person you want to be or the life you want to have? If it's a move toward, then invite guilt along as you engage in your healthy habit. Guilt is coming anyway, so you might as well not struggle with it. Welcome guilt as your smelly old companion, or perhaps a rambunctious puppy, but stick to your route.

Choice Point

On the choice point worksheet, beside "feelings" in the "passengers that get in the way" box, you might want to add some of the typical emotion passengers that show up for you so you can be more aware of them. I would record guilt, because it's one of the common emotion passengers that shows up for me when I try to go to the gym. You can also add some of the skills (making a peace treaty, feelings are the weather, taking guilt for a run) you learned in this chapter that can help you manage emotion passengers. Taking guilt for a run is a skill that works well for me when I'm trying to go to the gym, so I'd record that in the "skills" box. I welcome my guilt and bring it with me.

As with all skills, you need to practice them to do them well. I recommend making it a goal this week to practice one of the skills you learned. Keep in mind that your passengers will try to "help" you by suggesting that you avoid practicing these skills. For example, my client Charlie was working on accepting his feelings, and in one session he made the plan to practice checking in on them before the next session. When he returned and we checked in on his practice, we uncovered how his passengers had hampered his efforts:

Me: What did you notice while practicing checking in on your feelings?

Charlie: Oh, I forgot.

Me: Okay, how did the passengers help you forget?

Charlie: Oh, well, I thought about it but then I forgot.

Me: What do you think would have happened if the passengers hadn't helped you forget?

Charlie: I think I would have felt bad if I actually checked in on my anxiety, so I guess in a way they helped me not have to feel bad.

Me: Wow! Great noticing.

Even though his passengers had prevented him from practicing the skill of checking in, he was still able to notice how the passengers had taken him on a detour. Your passengers will help you avoid your feelings using any means necessary. Try to notice your passengers' efforts, thank them very much, and practice your skills for managing feelings anyway. Remember, doing so is about your *willingness* to feel bad in the service of your values.

CHAPTER 5

Be Glad You Don't Put Your Socks on like a Two-Year-Old

Imagine that, for some reason, you end up locking your dog out of the house and it's raining, and your poor dog sits outside in the rain all day. When you get back home and let him into the house, how does your dog respond? Most people will say that the dog will wag his tail and greet them and be just delighted that they're home. Now imagine that, for some reason, you end up locking your spouse (or your mom or dad or sister) out of the house and it's raining. When you get back home and let him or her into the house, how does your spouse (or mom or dad or sister) respond? Is your spouse happy to see you? Probably not.

Why do your dog and your spouse respond differently? Humans have the ability to represent experiences with symbolic language or thought. *Thinking* allows us to envision and experience things beyond what our five sense are experiencing in the present moment. Take the example of the dog. As soon as you come home and let him into the house, he's experiencing being in the house and you being home and he's happy. Because of symbolic language or thought, however, humans have the ability to exist in the past and the future regardless of what's going on in the present. The human can remember being outside all day long in the rain, and when you get home, this person is mad. Even once inside the house, the human is still experiencing being stuck out in the rain.

Symbolic thought and language have tremendous advantages. One is that learning doesn't require experience. Here's what I mean. With words alone you can teach a child that snakes are dangerous; the child never has to experience being bitten by a snake. This is clearly advantageous: humans can adapt and learn through language and don't require direct experience.

However, this ability also has a downside. What happens when you read the word "milk"? Perhaps images of white, cold liquid, or cookies, or cows, appear in your mind, or thoughts about whether you like milk or not. And all of this can happen without milk actually being present. This is the power of symbolic thought and language. We can experience things that aren't actually happening in the here and now. This ability for thoughts to be experienced as real can keep us from doing the things that matter to us in life. Thoughts like *I'm too tired to go to the gym* or *I really need a smoke* can be experienced as "real" and "true," whether or not they are, and interfere with our ability to stick to our healthy habits. In this chapter we're going to learn about how our thoughts impact us and how to still live our healthiest life and do the things that matter to us.

Automatic Pilot

Have you ever driven somewhere and then had no idea how you got there? Me too. Things like this happen when we're on automatic pilot. For example, one day while driving to work I ended up at my son's school, and he wasn't even in the car! My mind was on automatic pilot. This was a harmless event in which I fell into a routine habit, but if we allow ourselves to be on automatic pilot too much, it can also interfere with our ability to stick to our healthy habits.

Automatic pilot plays a big role in healthy habits, or lack thereof. Many of my clients living with obesity would tell the same tale of ending up on the couch in front of the TV eating potato chips and having little idea how they got there. I might press them, asking, "What were you thinking? What were you feeling?" The answers were often similar: "I don't know—it just happened." And I believe them. This is a classic example of being on automatic pilot, and none of us are immune. We get home from a long day, we're tired, and automatic pilot takes over and we do what we usually do. In fact, your mind has probably devised lovely ways for you to "treat" yourself at the end of a long day, such as having a drink, having a cigarette, or mindlessly eating junk food in front of the TV. Unfortunately, these behaviors have only short-term benefits. If you're not paying attention, automatic pilot can take you places you don't want to go, whether that's going to school when you meant to go to work or eating chips when you meant to be sticking to your healthy habits.

Automatic pilot isn't necessarily a bad thing, though. Have you ever watched a two-year-old try to put on socks? It is a long ordeal. And how about you? How long did it take you to put your socks on this morning? Do you even remember putting them on? Or did they somehow just end up on your feet? This is one of the benefits of automatic pilot. Processes like putting on socks have become nearly unconscious acts. Automatic pilot can relieve us of the need to process everything, freeing us up to think about other things. Imagine if it still took you as long to put on your socks as it does a two-year-old. You wouldn't have time for much else in your day. So automatic pilot can be great, but in order to stick to our route in life we also need to be able to turn it *off.*

Mindfulness

Mindfulness is the opposite of automatic pilot. It means paying attention to the present moment, on purpose, in a kind and nonjudgmental way (Kabat-Zinn 2016). Sometimes people ask me what the difference is between mindfulness and meditation. There are many different kinds of meditation, and many are attached to religious traditions or philosophies, such as Buddhism or Hinduism. One form is called mindfulness meditation. There are many different ways to practice mindfulness skills, only one of which is mindfulness meditation, and we'll review a variety of them in this chapter.

There are a few key skills involved in being mindful: observing our thoughts rather than getting caught up in them, doing this without judgment, and being in the present moment. We need to be able to turn off automatic pilot when doing so would help us with our health behaviors, and the skill of mindfulness is one way we can do this. It is a key skill for managing the thoughts that can get in the way of our healthy habits.

Many people erroneously think that "mindfulness" means "having no thoughts" or "having an empty mind." I've had clients say they can't practice mindfulness because their "minds are too busy" or they "can't turn off their thoughts." Mindfulness isn't about having an empty mind, it's about being able to notice and observe our thoughts rather than getting taken away by them. The practice of mindfulness entails noticing your mind wandering and then bringing it back to the present moment. It's not about preventing your mind from wandering, because a wandering mind is a normal thing.

A client of mine, Shannon, offered a great example of how she would get caught up in her thoughts and get taken away by them: "I'm trying to study for an exam, and I suddenly think 'How old is Beyoncé?' And then immediately I find myself googling her, and before I know it, I've spent twenty minutes looking up facts about her rather than studying for my exam." What her wandering mind did is normal. The goal is not to prevent the mind from wandering, but to notice when it has wandered and to bring it back.

One way to think about this process is to imagine that your thoughts are a football that your mind hands you. You can either take the football and run or you can drop it. Shannon's mind offered her the football of "How old is Beyoncé?" and she ran with it: *How old is Beyoncé? I thought she was older than me but maybe not. Google! Oh, look how old her kids are   ...* Mindfulness is dropping the football: *Oh, look! My mind is wandering. Let's come back to studying.*

Mindfulness is also not meant to be a relaxation exercise, as some people think. Some people feel relaxed or centered after practicing mindfulness, but this is only a bonus, not the goal. Talking about mindfulness is a bit like talking about dancing: it's not the same as experiencing dancing, and no matter how much you talk about dancing, it won't capture the experience itself. In the same way, it's a lot more clarifying to experience mindfulness firsthand. Let's review some skills or methods you can use to become more mindful.

Leaves on a Stream

Let's try a classic acceptance and commitment therapy mindfulness exercise (inspired by Harris 2009). There's an audio version available for download at this book's website: http://www.newharbinger.com/43317. Before we begin, take a moment to reflect on how your passengers might stop you from actually trying this exercise, thus knocking you off your route. Notice what they're saying. Try thanking the passengers for sharing, and then do the exercise anyway.

Imagine that you're standing by the side of a stream, and there are leaves floating by. Imagine this however you'd like. Now when you notice yourself having a thought, put that thought on a leaf and watch it float down the stream. If you have no thoughts, just picture the stream.

From time to time you will get caught up in a thought. This is normal and natural. When it happens, try to notice that you've been pulled away from the present moment, and gently bring yourself back to standing by the stream.

Perhaps you notice thoughts like *What kind of thought am I having?* or *Am I doing this exercise correctly?* Great noticing. Just put those thoughts on a leaf and watch them float by.

You're not trying to wash away your thoughts. Sometimes thoughts will get stuck in a little whirlpool. That's okay.

Perhaps you notice thoughts like *How long do I need to do this?* or *What am I supposed to get out of this?* or *What am I going to make for dinner?* Just place those thoughts on a leaf and watch them float down the stream.

Over and over again your mind will wander. Your job is just to notice that it has wandered and to gently bring yourself back to standing by the side of the stream, observing the water and leaves.

Take a moment to reflect on the experience you had while doing this exercise. What did you notice? Could you imagine yourself by the stream? Could you notice when your mind had wandered? Could you bring it back? Did you notice your mind judging your performance or commenting on the exercise? Whatever your experience was, it's okay. You're not trying to be perfect or to get it "right." You're just trying to increase your ability to notice when your mind has wandered and to bring it back.

Be the Weather Forecaster

Have you ever watched a weather report about a hurricane? Usually there's a reporter on the ground being pushed around by the wind, being pelted with rain, and yelling descriptions into the microphone like "strong winds" and "heavy rain." Then the broadcast returns to the weather forecaster in the studio who's standing in front of a satellite image of the hurricane. You can see the standard white swirl of the hurricane over blue water. The person calmly describes the direction of the wind and where the storm is headed. Both people are describing the same event, but their experiences are much different because their perspectives are different. The reporter on the ground is *caught up* in the storm, whereas the forecaster in the studio is *watching* or *observing* the storm.

This ability to achieve an observer perspective with our thoughts is a helpful way to become more mindful. We can get caught up in our thoughts (debating, analyzing, thinking) or we can observe them (like watching leaves on a stream or a hurricane from a studio).

There are a lot of different images you can employ to practice using this observer perspective. Thoughts naturally move, so any image involving you watching or observing your thoughts in motion is good. Common ones include clouds in the sky, a freight car going by, or packages on a conveyor belt. If we just get out of the way, a thought will naturally move along and be replaced by new thoughts, like the headlines passing along the banner of a CNN broadcast. If you miss a thought, don't worry! Your mind will remind you of it again. You can use the mindfulness exercise we just tried to find the observer perspective, replacing the leaves on a stream with imagery of your choice.

Another way to get into the observer perspective is to simply add "I notice I'm having the thought that..." to the front of a thought (Hayes, Strosahl, and Wilson 1999). A few weeks ago, I kept thinking *I'm exhausted,* and this thought affected my behavior, leading me to lie on the couch and watch random TV shows. This did not help me feel more energetic. The thought didn't lead me to eat better or go to bed earlier. In fact, I did the opposite: I ordered food in because I was "too exhausted" to cook, and I stayed up later, which made me want to sleep in each morning. I found myself getting further behind in my work and feeling more and more overwhelmed. Finally I realized that the thought wasn't helping me move toward my values, and I needed to do something about it.

I began by noticing the thought. Every time it came up, I said to myself, *I notice I'm having the thought that I'm exhausted. How interesting,* I thought. *There it is again.* As the week progressed and I kept noticing my thoughts, I got off the couch, I started getting to bed on time, and I made more homemade meals. Notice that I didn't change the thought or convince myself I wasn't exhausted. I just practiced noticing the thought so that I could stick with my healthy habits. Now if that thought had helped me take better care of myself, go to bed on time, or eat healthier, then I would have kept following it. But it didn't. It moved me away from my values. My job was to notice and observe it so I could do the things that mattered to me in the moment.

Present-Moment Awareness

Minds are awesome at being in the past (for example, that container of ice cream that you ate last night that you're now regretting) and being in the future (for example, worrying about how to get through Thanksgiving dinner with your family). While this is an amazing human ability, it can get us into trouble when we're trying to stick with healthy habits. Instead of being in the present we're caught up trying to solve past "mistakes" or plan for future outcomes. This can be frustrating, because you can't change the past or predict the future. Here's an example of how the mind can take us away from the present moment and create distress.

I was working with a client who had end-stage liver disease that required him to engage in a number of healthy habits (for example, a low-sodium high-protein diet, no processed foods, regular blood work, regular activity to reduce swelling, and so on). He had worked very hard to stick to these healthy habits so that he'd be eligible for a transplant. One day he came to session with great news: his doctors had decided to approve and list him for transplant. I asked him how he felt about this; he had been waiting a long time to get listed and had worked very hard for it. He said, "Well, I'm really worried about what happens when the transplant fails. What am I going to do then?" *What?!* I thought. He hadn't even gotten the transplant and his mind was already worried about what would happen if it failed!

So rather than enjoying this moment he had worked so hard to achieve, his mind was already many years in the future problem solving something that hadn't yet happened (and might never happen). And as a result, he felt overwhelmed and discouraged, despite getting good news. Moreover, this thinking actually *decreased* his ability to stick to his healthy habits. We then spent a lot of time working on mindfulness, practicing having him come back to the present moment so he could experience whatever was going on right now. Usually in the "right now" the things he needed to do felt doable. Let's try another exercise to practice being more mindful, which involves staying in the present moment.

Notice Your Five Senses

If you're feeling overwhelmed with the past or the future, you can focus on your five senses or your breath to bring yourself back to the present moment (Harris 2009). This skill can help you focus on your healthy habit and what you need to do right now. Our five senses and breath are always grounded right here in this moment. What do I mean? You can't smell something from five years ago. You can *remember* what it smelled like, but you can't *resmell* it. You can't taste something two years in the future. You can *imagine* what it will taste like, but you can't *taste* it. You can't rebreathe the breath you just inhaled. And so on. Whenever we notice our five senses or our breath, we can anchor ourselves to this moment—that is, we can be mindful. It's a straightforward exercise, even if it's not "easy."

Notice two things you can see. (For example, "I can see the gray floor." "I can see my black pants.")

Notice two things you can feel. (For example, "I can feel my legs touching the chair." "I can feel my toes in my shoes.")

Notice two things you can hear. (For example, "I can hear the cars outside." "I can hear the hum of the building.")

Whenever you are noticing these senses you are here in this moment. But just wait, your mind will pull you away again. This is normal. When it does, see if you can bring yourself back to this moment by noticing your senses:

I can feel my chest rising and falling.

I can feel my fingers touching each other.

And your mind will pull you away again ... *What am I going to make for dinner?* Again, this is totally normal. Try to bring yourself back to this moment:

I can hear the cars outside.

I can smell someone's cologne.

A key part of being mindful is to be nonjudgmental about what you are sensing in the present moment. Try not to judge whether the cars are too noisy or whether you like the color of the carpet. Judgments are actually just more thoughts that can pull you away from the present moment. Try to simply *observe* the things you can sense.

What was that like to bring yourself back to the present moment with your five senses or your breath? Did you notice your mind pulling you away? Bringing yourself back to the here and now is a valuable skill for being more mindful and sticking with what you need to do to be healthy right here, right now, rather than focusing on the past or the future.

Mindfulness Takes Practice

There are many ways to be more mindful, such as by observing your thoughts or by noticing your five senses. These skills are simple concepts but they aren't necessarily easy. Many of us are used to getting caught up in our thoughts all day long in order to live our lives. We think about getting up and going to work. We think about our tasks at work and use our thoughts to get our work done. In fact, it's often the very successful, high-functioning, and well-educated people who have the most difficult time adopting this observer perspective. Why? I think it's because their thoughts are so useful to their work that they don't have a lot of practice just noticing them. So if you're struggling with being mindful, with the observer perspective, and with being in the present moment, be kind to yourself. It's likely because your thoughts have been very useful to you. But the more you practice these skills, the better you'll get.

You might be thinking, *Great, I'm totally going to be mindful the next time I feel anxious.* If that's your plan, it definitely won't work. You don't plan your fire escape route during a fire. If you want mindfulness to work in a "hot," difficult situation, you need to practice a lot beforehand. You need to know your escape route long before the rooms are filling with smoke.

There are lots of ways you can practice mindfulness. You can informally practice any of the skills we went over. For example, try noticing your five senses during an activity that you usually do on automatic pilot. Morning routines provide great opportunities because many of us do a lot of activities (like putting on socks) while on automatic pilot. When was the last time you noticed the smell of your shampoo or the taste of your toothpaste? Being mindful isn't meant to make things take more time. In fact, it might reduce the amount of time it takes you to do things. For example, if you're mindful while you wash your hair instead of doing it on autopilot, you won't end up washing it twice if you forget whether or not you already washed it! Mindfulness is a skill you can improve by being more present more often.

And, of course, if you want to do formal mindfulness activities, like the leaves on a stream exercise, there's an app for that. In fact, there are many, many well-designed mindfulness apps. If you look for an app, I recommend picking one that starts with short (say, three minutes) mindfulness activities, so you can start developing your skills from a manageable place (remember our 90 percent rule).

Practicing mindfulness activities can help you learn how to notice your thoughts and not get caught up in them (or as psychotherapists say, "unhook" from your thoughts) when it's not helpful or they're moving you away from your values. When your thoughts move you toward your values it can be helpful to get caught up in them (for example, *I should get up and go to work.*) The goal is not to have fewer thoughts. The goal is to improve your ability to unhook from unhelpful ones. Remember the football metaphor from earlier in the chapter? You can either run with the football (your thoughts) or drop it. Some thoughts are harder to drop than others, because some thoughts are just stickier. The thought *I don't have time for that* is much stickier for me than *What will I make for dinner?* I had to practice unhooking from it because it was constantly causing me to deviate from my route. Over time thoughts can become less sticky, but they will never go away. Having mindfulness as a skill won't allow you to get rid of your passengers, but it will help you stick to your healthy habits route more often.

How Passengers Will Help Keep You Stuck

Your passengers probably won't be interested in you practicing mindfulness. Passengers are awesome at convincing us not to try new skills, even if these new skills might be helpful. What buttons do you think your passenger will try to press to convince you not to practice mindfulness? Let's look at a few common ways they might try to get to you.

But It's True

Passengers are very good at trying to convince us that our thoughts are true and therefore we must follow them. For example, if you're like me, you regularly have the thought *I don't have time for that.* When I try to be mindful and observe that thought, my passengers immediately offer "But it's true!" Do I really not have time, or are my passengers just wanting me to avoid trying something new that might move me toward my values?

A problem with using "the truth" as a guide for our decisions is that it's often impossible to tell whether a thought is "true" or not. Are you really too tired to go to the gym? Do you really not have time to make a lunch? The answers to these questions are subjective. There's no official test to find out if they're true or not. Minds can justify *anything!* Our passengers are great at taking over the bus and convincing us that a particular thought is "true," and therefore we must follow it.

But let's say that somehow you could prove a thought was true. Then does that mean you should follow the thought? Let's try a thought experiment (inspired by Harris 2009). Consider the thought *Someday I will die.* Most of us agree that this is a true thought, but getting caught up in it might not help you. Perhaps you'll end up thinking about how dangerous life is, and in order to avoid dangerous things you won't want to leave the house. Or perhaps you'll reason that since you're going to die anyway, you might as well live life to the fullest and drink and smoke and eat whatever you want. Either response is not likely to move you toward your values.

So rather than debating with yourself about whether the thought you're having is true or not, ask if the thought will move you toward or away from your values. If it will move you toward them, then great. Follow it! If it will move you away from them, then thank those passengers very much for sharing and move toward your values anyway.

I Forgot

Another very effective way that passengers will keep you from trying something new is to help you forget. Over and over again, when clients and I set the goal for them to practice mindfulness (or some other new skill), they come to session the following week and say, "I forgot to do it."

Setting a reminder is an obvious way to not forget to do something, but it doesn't always work. Clients often ask me, "Can I get an app to remind myself to be mindful?" Of course you can!

There are many mindfulness apps that will send you little reminders throughout the day to notice your toes or to take a deep breath. In fact, I have several of them on my smartphone. And what do you think happens when that mindfulness reminder on my phone pops up? I dismiss it. I don't stop to be mindful. And this is, in part, because my passengers have helped me code this reminder as "not important."

What do you think I do when the phone number for my son's school shows up on my phone? That's right: I answer the phone! It doesn't matter if I'm driving or I'm in a meeting or I'm with a client, I don't dismiss it. This number has been coded as "important," as something I need to attend to in order to be a "good parent." This behavior is probably related to my cave person brain that's on alert for danger. However, being mindful may be just as important to being a "good parent" as answering the phone is when the school calls. If I practice being more mindful, then I'm more present with my son when we're together.

So, to stick to our route, we need to find a way to actively recode the things our passengers deem "unimportant" (such as practicing mindfulness) as "important." A way to do this is to remind yourself of the value that a particular behavior is helping you express. For example, practicing mindfulness can be an expression of my value of being an engaged parent. Here's another example.

One of my clients with diabetes had many, *many* reminders to engage in healthy habits. And just like me he tended to ignore or dismiss them. For example, he wanted to get better at cleaning the house with regularity. Because of his diabetes he was unable to work, so his wife earned the income for their family. Cleaning the house was one way that he could support his wife. When we talked about what got in the way of cleaning, he said, "I think about it in the morning. But then I get to doing other things and I completely forget." Well done, passengers!

First, I had him delete all the reminders on his phone (he wasn't paying attention to them anyway), and then we established only one daily reminder on his phone: "Be a good husband: clean the house." We deliberately coded this reminder as "important" by including the value that was associated with the behavior. By our next session he was proud to report that he'd spent time cleaning the house every day, and that his wife was also very pleased.

Mindfulness in Action

So here is the task, if you're willing. Set yourself the goal of practicing mindfulness regularly (remember the 90 percent rule when deciding how much mindfulness you should practice; as an ultimate goal, fifteen minutes per day might be reasonable), and do one of the following: either spend time doing one of the mindfulness exercises from this chapter, or notice what got in the way of you practicing mindfulness. That is, what did the passengers have to say or do to stop you from trying something new? Did they help you forget? Did they tell you that you don't have time for such things? Did they tell you that mindfulness wasn't going to work or that you wouldn't stick with it, so why bother? Noticing what gets in the way or actually practicing mindfulness is going to help you be more in charge of your bus. And when you're in charge of your bus, you're more likely to engage in health behaviors. You can use the "Practicing Mindfulness" worksheet, available for download at this book's website (http://www.newha rbinger.com/43317), to record your experiences.

Choice Point

Having read this chapter, you can add a few new things to the choice point worksheet. You can write in some common "thought passengers" that get in the way of your healthy habits. For example, *I don't have time for that* is one thought that often shows up for me when I try to go to the gym, so I would write that next to "thoughts" at the bottom left. You can also list some of the mindfulness skills (leaves on a stream, observer perspective, present-moment awareness, notice your five senses) that we covered—and you have now practiced—under "skills." I often use "I notice I'm having the thought that..." to help me manage my thought passengers that are related to going to the gym—as in *I notice I'm having the thought that I don't have time for that.* Try practicing some of these mindfulness skills over the next week.

CHAPTER 6

I Suck at Being Compassionate with Myself

Have you ever had the experience of replaying a painful or difficult experience from the past, such as when you forgot your lines in the school play, when you tripped in the cafeteria, or when you couldn't think of anything useful to say at the party and everyone thought you were stupid? I'm willing to bet the answer is yes. Our brain is hardwired to replay painful experiences for us. This trait was very helpful for cave people, because those who didn't look for danger, for what was wrong, for what needed fixing, and for what was lacking were less likely to survive. If you were a cave person and you survived a bear attack, then it would have been really useful to remember how you survived the attack, and you'd definitely want to be on the lookout for more bears. Imagine the opposite scenario: a cave person is attacked by a bear and survives and then *completely forgets* that it happened or how he saved himself. This person is not our ancestor.

Research suggests that social-emotional pain (for example, being embarrassed at a party) and physical pain (for example, spraining your ankle) are stored in the same place in our brain, meaning our brain doesn't distinguish between the two (Eisenberger, Lieberman, and Williams 2003). Both are remembered as pain and something to be avoided. This is why our mind reminds us of social-emotional painful experiences even though there's not much to learn from this rehashing. It's what our brain has evolved to do—remember painful experiences in order to avoid them. Unfortunately, replaying a painful experience isn't likely to help you prevent the same experience from happening in the future. That's not to say you can't learn from your social-emotional "mistakes," but any information you get out of that experience will likely happen right away. Rehashing it weeks later is unlikely to be helpful.

Comparing ourselves to others is another trait we got from our cave people ancestors (Harris 2008). Cave people would not have survived on their own. They needed the protection, support, and resources of the tribe. So our mind evolved to watch out for signs that we might get kicked out of the tribe. *Am I too different from the others? Am I contributing enough? Am I good enough for the tribe?* In our modern world we have millions of people to compare ourselves to, which leads many of us to constantly feel we're not enough of ... something. This tendency to compare ourselves to others often takes the form of a "self-critical" passenger.

For example, did you know that I'm not blond enough? And I'm definitely not tall enough or pretty enough or thin enough. Well, that's what my self-critical passenger tells me all the time. We all have an "I'm not good enough" story like this. It might be that you're not smart enough or thin enough or wealthy enough or kind enough or ambitious enough. This "I'm not good enough" story is typical of the self-critical passenger, a regular on the bus who descended from this ancient part of the brain. Remember, cave people who didn't look for what was wrong, for what needed fixing, and for what was lacking were less likely to survive.

Unfortunately, there's no way to turn off this self-critical part of the brain. The choice we have is how long do we want to hang out in that place of self-criticism. How far do we want to run with the self-critical football? How often do we want to let that self-critical passenger drive our bus? There is an antidote to the self-critical passenger. Self-compassion can help us disarm this passenger.

In Western culture, many people mistakenly believe that the self-critical passenger is useful, that it can motivate us to be better people. If we're hard on ourselves we're more likely to improve. Research actually shows the opposite. Numerous studies have found that self-compassion rather than self-criticism is more useful for motivating change (Zhang and Chen 2016), and therefore it's very useful for helping us stick to healthy habits.

Self-Compassion

Researcher Dr. Kristen Neff defines *self-compassion* as involving three main parts. The first is *self-kindness,* being kind, caring, and loving to oneself. The second is *common humanity,* recognizing that setbacks, personal feelings, and mistakes are all part of being human. And the third is *mindfulness,* being able to notice and be present in a nonjudgmental way (2003a, 2003b). According to Dr. Neff, self-compassion is not self-pity. With self-pity we're focused on the "Why me?" But that is the opposite of common humanity. Self-compassion is also not self-indulgence, nor is it self-esteem. Our culture is obsessed with self-esteem, which usually involves comparing ourselves to others and trying to downplay our faults in order to maintain high self-esteem. This is the opposite of recognizing that we all have faults and failings, which are aspects of common humanity.

Research suggests that self-compassion is linked to improved health, life satisfaction, and well-being and to lower anxiety, depression, and stress (Pinto–Gouveia et al. 2014; Hope, Koestner, and Milyavskaya 2014; MacBeth and Gumley 2012; Miyagawa and Taniguchi 2016; Neff 2003b; Neff, Rude, and Kirkpatrick 2007; Zessin, Dickhäuser, and Garbade 2015). Research also suggests that self-compassion is related to persistence while undertaking difficult tasks (Neff, Hsieh, and Dejitterat 2005; Hope, Koestner, and Milyavskaya 2014; Neely et al. 2009). For example, researchers conducted a study in which participants worked on a difficult math problem (Neff 2013). The researchers weren't interested in whether the participants could solve the math problem. In fact, the problem was unsolvable. They were interested in how much effort participants would put into trying to solve the math problem, or how much *persistence* they showed. The longer participants worked, the more persistence they showed. One group received self-compassion instructions first, and the other group regular instructions. Self-compassion instructions include things like "As you work on this math problem, try to be kind to yourself," or "Remember, this might be a difficult task for most people, not just you." The group that received the self-compassion instructions spent more time trying to solve the math problem. In other words, they persisted for a longer time at a difficult task. Thus, the study linked self-compassion with persistence when faced with difficult tasks. And you know that engaging in any health behavior is a difficult task!

Self-compassion also helps us persist in the face of mistakes and setbacks, all of which we will face in our efforts to be healthy. So our ability to be compassionate is a critical skill for helping us stick with healthy habits. Let's look at some skills we can employ to be kinder to ourselves.

The Best Teachers

Western culture espouses this idea that to motivate yourself you need to be hard on yourself, even though research clearly shows this isn't the case. Let's try an exercise (inspired by Gilbert, Tirch, and Silberstein 2017) to examine this idea.

Imagine that self-critical passenger. Imagine what that harsh, mean criticism sounds like. Now imagine what that self-critical passenger looks like? If it was a being standing in front of you, what would it look like? People often describe their self-critical passenger as a monster, the devil, a troll, a dragon, a warlord, or a witch.

Now imagine a school filled with self-critical passengers, and they are the teachers in this school. So when you walk down the hallway you see monsters, trolls, devils, dragons, warlords, and witches. Would you want to go to this school? Would you learn well from these teachers? Would you send your child to this school? Would you want these figures teaching your child?

Now imagine a kind, compassionate passenger. This passenger has a soft voice and is kind and caring and always accepts you as you are. If you can imagine this compassionate passenger, what does it look like? People often describe an angel, a saint, a fairy godmother, a dove, a teddy bear, or a religious figure, such as Jesus, Buddha, and Mother Teresa.

Now imagine a school filled with compassionate passengers, and they are the teachers in this school. So when you walk down the hallway you see angels, saints, fairy godmothers, doves, teddy bears, Jesus, Buddha, and Mother Teresa. Would you want to go to this school? Would you learn well from such teachers? Would you be willing to send your child to this school? Would you be pleased to have these teachers instructing and shaping your child?

Most people agree that they wouldn't want to attend or send their kids to the school filled with self-critical passengers, much preferring the idea of the school filled with compassionate passengers. Although culturally we get the message that being hard on yourself will get you to change your ways and achieve more, our own experience, and scientific research, tells us the opposite.

Compassionate Hands

Let's take a moment now to practice self-compassion with this exercise adapted from Dr. Neff (2013).

Hold your hands out in front of you. Make them into fists. What do you notice? *(Most people say things like "tension.")*

Now open your hands with the palms facing the sky. What do you notice? *(Most people say things like "openness" or "relaxed.")*

Now put one hand over the other and place them both over your heart. What do you notice? *(Most people say things like "comfort," "warm," or "feels like a hug.")*

Did you actually do the exercise? When I first came across this exercise I thought to myself, *There's no way that's actually going to do anything.* My passengers told me not to bother trying it. If your passengers are doing the same, thank them for sharing, and then put your two hands over your heart anyway. Compassion often involves physical touch, which is one way we comfort children, so this simple act can be remarkable. I feel like I'm giving myself a hug. If it doesn't do anything for you, that's okay, just notice that. The other exercises in this chapter may speak to you more. I use this skill all the time, such as when I'm stressed, worried, overwhelmed, or frustrated.

Here's an example of how self-compassion can help you stick with healthy habits. At one point during my divorce I found out that my son had seven cavities, and one tooth was so bad that the dentist thought it might have to be pulled. It turned out that the Gatorade I was providing him (which my mind told me I *had* to give him because he *had* to stay hydrated because he refused to drink plain water) was giving him cavities. Well, that was part of it. Sometimes when my mind told me I was too exhausted to battle with him, I let him go to bed without brushing his teeth.

My self-critical passenger had a field day with this news: "You're a terrible mother. I can't believe you let this happen. What is wrong with you?!" These thoughts did not help move me toward being the kind of parent I wanted to be. Berating myself made me even more exhausted, so I had even less energy to battle my kid about Gatorade or brushing his teeth. Finally, I decided I needed to be compassionate with myself. Yes, things had fallen through the cracks while the divorce was happening, and I had taken some shortcuts because I was worn out. I knew that I was definitely not being the kind of parent I wanted to be, because I wanted to encourage healthy habits in my son, but I recognized that I was a human, and humans make mistakes.

So every time the self-critical passenger emerged I put my hands over my heart and reminded myself that I was doing my best in a difficult situation, and that it was okay. I would remind myself of my values, such as being a parent who encouraged healthy habits, and that we all struggle. The result was that I felt calmer and more in control. I was able to use my energy to battle my son's teeth brushing and Gatorade consumption rather than my own passengers. I couldn't get rid of the Gatorade all at once (remember the 90 percent rule), so I went from letting him drink as much as he wanted to one Gatorade per day. Then I only allowed him to drink it on days when he played sports, then once a week, and then I stopped buying Gatorade altogether. I made space for the discomfort of saying no to him.

When he went back to the dentist six months after the seven-cavity visit, he had no cavities. Being compassionate with myself gave me the strength to do the hard work necessary to get me (and him) to engage in health behaviors and move toward my values.

Compassionate Figure

Imagining a compassionate figure comforting you in moments of struggle can increase your ability to engage in self-compassion (inspired by Tirch, Schoendorff, and Silberstein 2014). A compassionate figure might be someone who has been really kind and caring toward you, perhaps an aunt, a grandparent, or a teacher. Pets are often great options because we often experience them as loving us with total acceptance. It's best not to pick a romantic partner or your parents because we often have complicated relationships with these people. Many of my clients often can't think of a compassionate figure in their lives. If that's true of you, too, a great alternative is to consider a character from a movie or a TV show, or a public figure. This person should be someone who just makes you smile. My clients have come up with all sorts of examples: Winnie the Pooh, Mary Poppins, Mother Teresa, Big Bird, the housekeeper from the TV show *Facts of*

Life, the mom from *The Brady Bunch,* or the fairy godmother from *Cinderella.*

Let's practice this skill. Think of a mistake you made, not the worst mistake ever, but something along the lines of a 3 or 4 out of 10. Think eating a whole pizza or having a cigarette at a party when you were trying to quit. Here's an example of mine. One time while driving to the airport my secretary called me to tell me that my three o'clock appointment had arrived. For whatever reason this appointment hadn't made it into my calendar. To make matters worse, the client was seeing me for a liver-transplant assessment and had traveled from New Brunswick—a five-hour drive. Immediately I felt awful: *How could I have done this? What am I going to do? This is so awful!* Even as I tell this story now I can feel a sinking in my stomach. Notice how my mind judged me? This is because I care about my clients and their suffering, and being reliable and helpful matters to me, neither of which had I accomplished with this client in this situation.

Now imagine your compassionate figure comes into the room and sits down next to you and recognizes that you're suffering. She places her hands on your leg or arm, or maybe puts her arms around you, and says, "I know you didn't want this to happen. I know this upsets you. I know you're suffering." Now imagine what that person would say to you about this mistake to comfort you. Perhaps your compassionate figure looks at you, with arms around you and tears in her eyes because she can see your pain, and says, "It's going to be okay. I'm here with you."

What was it like to hear a compassionate response to your mistake? What do you notice? Do you feel a bit calmer or comforted? Your compassionate figure doesn't need to actually be in the room with you for you to be able to bring some compassion into your life. That's because this compassionate person is in you. You can bring him or her forth whenever you need support. The next time you make a mistake (and you will, because you're human), bring forth your compassionate figure to give you some comfort. You can use the "Compassionate Figure" worksheet, available for download at this book's website (http://www.newharbinger.com /43317), to walk yourself through this exercise whenever you need to.

Loving-Kindness

You can also practice self-compassion through loving-kindness meditation. You can download an audio version of the following meditation (adapted from Bowen, Chawla, and Marlatt 2011) at this book's website: h ttp://www.newharbinger.com/43317.

Imagine someone who is easy to love, someone who brings a smile to your face. It's best not to choose people you've had conflict with or whom you are involved with romantically. It can be a pet or a child you know, or perhaps a TV or movie character, a public figure, or a compassionate figure you imagined in one of the earlier exercises.

Now imagine sending this person kind wishes, the way you'd wish someone a good day or safe travels. You could send them these well-wishes: may you be well, may you be healthy, may you live with ease. Or you can send wishes of your own devising that you feel comfortable with. Just send well-wishes to this person for a few moments.

Now imagine this person sending these same well-wishes to you. Imagine them saying to you, "May you be well, may you be healthy, may you live with ease." Notice what it feels like to receive these well-wishes. Where do these feelings show up in your body?

Now imagine sending these well-wishes to yourself: may I be well, may I be healthy, may I live with ease. Notice any resistance you feel to receiving these well-wishes. If it's easier, imagine yourself as a small child receiving them. See if you can thank your passengers who might be commenting on whether you deserve these wishes or not, and continue to send them to yourself for a few moments.

Many people with whom I've done this exercise notice that they're resistant to sending well-wishes to themselves. Perhaps you felt it too. This resistance may always be there, but it will become "less sticky" the more you practice self-compassion.

Self-Compassion Takes Practice

I've done similar self-compassion exercises with health care providers who are coping with medical mistakes. There's a good chance that most nurses and physicians can offer details about the first patient who died while under their care. There's a good chance they'll be able to walk you through that experience minute by minute, and that they still experience the pain of losing that patient even if it was more than thirty years ago. Sometimes they feel that the only instructions medical schools offered them about making mistakes was to not make them. There's no way to go back and "fix" the mistakes of the past, but health care providers who are able to be more compassionate with themselves, and who don't remain stuck in their heads criticizing themselves, notice that they are better able to pay attention to and be caring with current patients.

The same can be true of you and your mistakes, even if you're not dealing with life-and-death situations. So if your passengers are telling you that self-compassion might be okay if you're dealing with some small issue, like eating a whole pizza, but it won't help with the really big mistakes, then thank them for sharing. And then give yourself a hug for all your mistakes and failings, big and small.

Choice Point

Having read this chapter, you can now add "self-criticism" under "passengers that get in the way," and "self-compassion" under "skills," on the choice point worksheet. My self-criticism passenger often tells me how out of shape or fat I am or how going to the gym won't do any good anyway. In these moments I often put my hands over my heart and remind myself to be kind to myself so I can get to the gym. Going forward, remember that self-compassion is a skill you can practice. Pick one of the self-compassion exercises to try practicing this week. Don't forget to notice how your passengers try to take you off your route when you try to practice this new skill.

PART 3

Living a Healthy Life

CHAPTER 7

Get Yourself out of Solitary Confinement

In the United States, what do we do with the worst, most difficult prisoners? We put them in solitary confinement. It's hardly surprising that solitary confinement is a form of punishment, since evolutionarily we are hardwired to seek connection with other humans. Let's explore the reasons why this is the case.

A foal typically stands within thirty minutes of being born, and within a few hours it can run with the herd. Human babies, however, are incredibly reliant on caregivers for survival. The first three months after birth are often referred to as the "fourth trimester," meaning that babies really should still be in the womb. The reason they don't stay there longer is that at around forty weeks (nine months) the human skull is still small enough to pass through the birth canal. If we spend any more time in the womb, our mothers wouldn't be able to give birth to us. So being born "too soon" has been a necessary trade-off in human evolution: we get to have a large, adaptive brain, but we're born before we can survive on our own. As a result, humans take care of their young for longer than almost any other mammal (Tirch, Schoendorff, and Silberstein 2014).

Evolution needed a way to motivate caregivers to take care of these rather helpless newborns, and it came in the form of *attachment* (Cozolino 2010; Mikulincer and Shaver 2007b; Siegel 2012), which is the bond that develops between a baby and a caregiver (Bowlby 1969, 1973; Mikulincer and Shaver 2007a). Attachment is the reason we feel soothed and calm in the presence of safe and caring loved ones and distressed when we're separated from them (Porges 2007). These feelings go both ways for infants and caregivers. In fact, the sound of a crying baby motivates parents to care for infants, so much so that listening to a crying baby is sometimes used as a form of torture. Attachment also explains why solitary confinement (being separated from other humans) is a form of punishment. The effects of attachment don't end with the baby-parent relationship, as we carry these forward into our relationships with spouses and other important people in our life.

Western culture is fixated on the notions of individualism and independence. We receive messages that we need to "love ourselves" and to be able to "be on our own," and that it's dysfunctional to be dependent on others. The problem with these notions is that we're hardwired to function better when we have close, safe, and secure relationships with others. When we feel securely connected to others, we're better able to explore the world, handle challenges, and be resilient (Bowlby 1969, 1973; Mikulincer and Shaver 2007b). In fact, the Western world is in the minority with its focus on individualism. Most of the world focuses on collectivism, which prioritizes group cohesiveness and interdependence. Collectivistic cultures assume that close relationships are necessary for well-being.

Personally, I hate to be alone. I'm an extrovert, and I feel uneasy when I'm by myself for long periods of time. I used to think this made me weak or dysfunctional, and that I needed to learn to be more independent. But now that I understand human evolution better, I realize that my anxiousness about being alone is hardwired! It's not dysfunctional. That said, there clearly is a balance. It may not be healthy to be around people who are unsupportive or unkind just to avoid being alone.

So why am I talking about relationships in a book about health behaviors? Studies show that close relationships make us healthier. People's wounds heal faster if they have secure, close relationships, and they recover from illness faster, have a longer life, and are mentally healthier (for example, Holt-Lunstad, Smith, and Layton 2010).

When we're younger, having more people in our social network predicts better health, but as we mature the *quality* of relationships rather than the *quantity* matters more (Carmichael, Reis, and Duberstein 2015). So if you're reading this thinking *I don't have many good friends,* don't worry; having just one close relationship is enough for you to gain these health benefits. There's also evidence that how healthy your friends are predicts how healthy you are. For example, studies have shown that if your social network includes a lot of people living with obesity, there is a greater chance that you'll also be living with obesity (Christakis and Fowler 2007). There are multiple different reasons why the healthy habits of our family and friends might influence ours, including genetics, such as the propensity to put on weight or a preference for sugary foods; living in similar environments, such as those with access to parks and walking paths; and shared social norms, such as having social events that revolve around food (Hruschka et al. 2011; Bartle 2012). Thus, having a social network that focuses on healthy habits can be key to keeping your own healthy habits going.

No human is an island—at least the healthy ones aren't. Just as you don't live alone in a vacuum, your healthy habits don't happen in a vacuum either. People in your life can be both allies and foes (usually unintentionally) when it comes to how you live, so your social network plays a big role in your ability to engage in healthy habits and to live a healthy and vibrant life. In this chapter we're going to explore our close relationships and how to have your social environment support your healthy habits.

What to Do with Other People...

When I worked at the obesity clinic, I regularly heard stories from participants about how they worked hard to keep snacks like potato chips or chocolate out of their home only to have a spouse or children or a parent bring them back in. "How can I possibly be healthy when my husband keeps bringing potato chips into the house!? I've asked him a hundred times to stop, and he still does it." Dealing with other people is not a simple task. I could probably write a whole book on this topic alone. Here are a few ways you can deal with other people in your life (Harris 2009), each of which I'll go over in more detail:

- Change the things you can change.
- Accept the things you cannot change.
- Do nothing.
- Leave.

Change the Things You Can Change

If others in your social network are not supporting your healthy habits, the first step is to ask directly for their support. Assertiveness is a skill you can use to better communicate your needs and increase the likelihood that others in your life will support your healthy habits. There are lots of ways to define *assertiveness.* I have found it easiest to describe assertiveness (and the alternative ways to communicate) in political terms:

- *Assertive* communication is like a democracy: You get to have your vote, but your candidate doesn't always win. In other words, you get to state your needs but you don't always get your way.

- *Aggressive* communication is like a dictatorship: you say what you need and always get your way.

- *Passive* communication means you don't even vote (or state a need), which often results in your needs not being met.

- *Passive-aggressive* communication means you don't state your needs clearly but make sure you get your way. You don't vote (you don't state a need), but you still make sure you get the outcome you want. This communication style is like using espionage to throw a coup and put your own dictator in power.

Assertive communication involves clearly and directly expressing your feelings, opinions, and needs while respecting the feelings and rights of others. It's about you stating your needs, not about whether they get met or not. How you behave is within *your* control; how the other person responds is outside of your control. The only way you'll find out if people in your life can meet your needs is if you ask specifically for what you need. For example, there's a difference between saying, "I need to focus on my healthy habits, so I can't go to Ribfest with you," versus "I can't believe you're asking me to go to Ribfest!"

It's good to keep in mind that what you're asking of others may involve a difficult healthy habit for them too. When practicing assertive communication, it can help to apply all the things you've learned about changing healthy habits so far. For example, ask for a "do instead" goal rather than a "don't do" goal ("I'm trying to eat healthier these days. Can we go to a place that has a salad bar instead of a place that only serves fried food?"). Or perhaps you can use the 90 percent rule: "At least once this week can we eat at home instead of having fast food?"

What gets in the way. Changing your interpersonal style (the ways you relate to others) to be more assertive is a big task, because interpersonal styles are learned from a young age and for very important reasons. Because children can't choose their family or their environment, they have to adapt. Perhaps as a child you learned to put on a smile even when you were upset, or you were a people pleaser or learned that yelling was the only way to be heard. We all learned such adaptation strategies, and we can be grateful to our mind for figuring out ways for us to survive our childhood environments, some of which were probably pretty difficult.

But as adults we have more choice. We usually get to choose our partners, our friends, and our careers, so this method for survival may no longer be adaptive. It may not help you be healthier or live a life that matters to you. Unfortunately, once the mind finds a survival strategy that works, it wants to keep using it no matter what. So changing your interpersonal style probably goes against a well-learned and well-practiced survival strategy. Your passengers may yell at you, and you may need to drive over many rumble strips and feel all kinds of discomfort.

The good news is that you now have all kinds of skills to handle these passengers. (Just review the last few chapters!) Remember, if you find communicating more assertively to be difficult, please start by being compassionate with yourself. When you consider everything you know about yourself, your personality, your temperament, your family, and your childhood, your communication style probably makes complete sense. Remind yourself that you didn't choose how your mind adapted to past circumstances, and you didn't choose your parents or your childhood (Tirch, Silberstein, and Kolts 2018). It's not your fault you're struggling to change your communication style, but it is your responsibility, because no one else but you can choose to change.

Accept the Things You Cannot Change

Remember, being assertive means that you state your needs, not that your needs get met all the time. If your needs are getting met all the time, you're actually being aggressive, not assertive. There will be people in your life who, no matter how assertive you are, are not able to meet your needs. Many (but not all) of us experience this dynamic with the family we were born with. If you've struggled with your parents or siblings, assertiveness may do little to change the dynamics of these relationships.

Typically, if somebody is going to be able to meet your need, they will do so on your first or second request. If you're on your 147th request, it's unlikely this person will be able to meet your need. Now if you're a well-functioning human, your problem-solving mind is going to go to work on changing this person. *Why is he behaving this way? What do I need to say to get her to stop? Maybe if I say it at the right time ... Maybe if I say it with the right words ... Maybe if I explain it again so she gets it ...* Here's the thing: we can't control other people, but your mind will still do its problem-solving thing and try to figure out how to "solve" the other person's behavior, but this strategy does not work. We can't "fix" or "solve" other people.

So then what? The best strategy is to accept that your need will not be met by this person, whom you can't control. Again, "accept" doesn't mean giving in or giving up. It doesn't mean liking or enjoying it. Accepting means taking what is given, moving from "How do I get this person to change" to "*Given* that this person is not going to change, what do I want to do?" Thus, rather than figuring out how to get your partner to stop bringing potato chips into the house, you move to, *Given that my partner won't stop bringing potato chips into the house, how am I going to deal with it?* You may notice that at this point your mind very helpfully suggests some other problem-solving fix to get your partner to change. Just thank your mind and redirect the problem-solving energy toward things you can control, such as *your* behavior. For example, if potato chips in the house is a problem, be sure to have a bag of kale chips in the house to snack on when the urge to eat the potato chips arises. And honor your own feelings of being disappointed that this person in your life cannot meet your needs: this means acknowledging and taking care of your feelings even if other people are not considering your feelings. (Remember checking in on your puppy—that is, your feelings?)

How to cope. Problem-focused coping and emotion-focused coping are the two main forms of coping we engage in (Carver, Scheier, Weintraub 1989). Problem-focused coping is often effective when the stressor or problem can be fixed or eliminated, and many of us use it in our day-to-day lives. For example, when you have a deadline at work you focus harder on the tasks at hand to complete the project on time, and the problem is fixed. Emotion-focused coping is often effective when the stressor or problem can't be fixed or eliminated. It involves managing the feelings that arise from the stressor rather than getting rid of the stressor itself. This form of coping is more effective when we need to deal with people who cannot meet our needs.

One emotion-focused coping strategy is to "refuel." A refueling activity is one that makes you feel *more* energetic once you've done it. Sometimes we do things that we think are relaxing (for example, watching TV) but are actually just a form of zoning out. These activities can actually make us feel more tired. Here are some common refueling activities:

- Spending time with friends and family
- Playing sports
- Meditation
- Going to church
- Getting a massage
- Doing yoga
- Listening to music
- Taking a hot shower
- Walking the dog
- Doing a hobby or crafts

Different things refuel different people, so you get to choose activities that match your preferences and values. If you're not sure what does or will work, try some out and notice what shows up. Do you feel energized after playing a board game with your kid, going for a hike, or having coffee with a friend? If so, then these are refueling activities for you. And, as always, notice how your passengers may try to dissuade you from engaging in refueling activities. If a passenger says, "You don't have time for that," thank her and do it anyway!

Do Nothing

Sometimes we do nothing because our passengers are in charge of our bus and they have convinced us that it doesn't matter what we do. We can't change things, so why bother. But sometimes we do nothing because we decide that some other value is more important than changing the situation we're in.

For example, I worked with a nurse who felt the hospital unit she worked in was unhealthy and toxic. She felt stressed all the time and never had time to take care of herself. Yet she decided to stay because the position gave her health care benefits, and she had a sick child to care for. It is okay to make a decision like this if it is truly consistent with your values. She and I worked on redirecting the energy she put into changing her workplace toward the things that mattered to her, such as being with her sick child, and toward the things she had control over. For example, we made sure she was engaging in refueling activities, because the stressors in her workplace were going to remain and would likely deplete her energy. If, like this nurse, you decide to do nothing about a relationship or situation, I encourage you to review the section "Accept the Things You Cannot Change" so you can "do nothing" in the most effective way.

There may also be relationships you can't leave. You will always be a daughter or son. One of my clients, Katie, had a very difficult relationship with her father, and spending time with him sapped her energy and resulted in her not taking care of herself. She chose to accept that she wasn't going to have the kind of relationship she really wanted with her father, and to limit her contact with him. We spent a lot of time honoring her feelings of sadness and disappointment. That is, we worked on getting in touch with her feelings and taking care of them. Another client, Marie, couldn't stop her parents from visiting despite the negative effect it had on her healthy habits. Her parents always brought cake when they visited, and she always ended up eating it to cope with her mother's criticism. We developed ways that she could control her contact with them, rather than having it be the way they wanted it. She decided to visit them on a regular schedule (Sundays for two hours after church), and between this scheduled time she limited her contact with her parents, reminding them that she would see them on Sunday.

Leave

Sometimes lifestyle change means leaving a toxic workplace or ending an unsupportive relationship. If others in your life can't meet your needs, you may need to develop new relationships with people who can meet your needs. If you decide that you need to leave an unhelpful situation or relationship, your passengers will try to stop you (remember, the devil you do know is better than the devil you don't know), so be prepared for rumble strips ahead! Be ready for your passengers by answering these questions well in advance of any change you make: What value will I be expressing by leaving this relationship or environment? How will leaving this situation help me be the person I want to be? How will I manage the passengers and the discomfort that will arise in order to move toward this value?

Is There Someone in Your Boat?

There will be many things in life that you can't solve. People in your life may not behave the way you want them to, your body may not do what you want it to do, and life circumstances will keep getting in the way of your heathy habits. Close, secure relationships can really help you cope with these realities.

Let's do another thought experiment. Imagine you're in a little rowboat out on the ocean, and the boat is taking on water. Other people are worried about the boat sinking, and they attempt to help you in different ways. Some people stand on the shore and shout instructions: "Maybe if you bailed faster," or "Try bailing with both hands." These folks are trying to "fix" your problem. Here's a real-world example. Let's say you've been struggling to quit smoking, and a friend says, "Have you tried that gum? I heard it works. Did you try hypnosis? Maybe that will work." Your friend is probably saying this with the best intentions, but if the problem could be fixed that easily you would have fixed it already. It's likely that your problem has no fix or involves a messy, complicated fix, such as needing to manage your passengers more effectively.

Sometimes people paddle out in a boat and get beside you, saying things like "I know how bad that must be, I've been in a sinking boat too." In the real world, it might look something like this: You're describing to a friend your lifelong struggle with weight, and she responds, "Oh, I know. It took me over a year to lose my baby weight with the last baby, but just keep working at it." She's trying to be helpful, trying to make you feel better, but hearing about another's personal experience sometimes feels like it takes away from our experience.

Then there are people who get in the boat with you. These people don't help you bail; they don't try to fix the problem. What they do is help you feel less alone. Your problem doesn't go away, but the pain you feel is more bearable when you're not alone.

Getting in the boat involves validating someone's experience, which is not the same as validating that the other person's beliefs are correct. Saying, "I can understand why your weight bothers you" is not the same as saying "You're right; you're overweight and your life is terrible." We often try to talk someone down (make them feel better) by telling them something's not that bad, but this often results in them upping the ante—that is, they describe something that's even worse.

Here's an example:

Anna: I hate this medication for my diabetes. I wish I didn't have to take it.

Jane: Oh, I'm sure it's not that bad. Just stick with it.

Anna: No, you clearly don't understand. It's really bad. It makes me tired and nauseous and I don't think it's even helping.

Jane: Well, I'm sure the doctors wouldn't give it to you if it wasn't helpful.

Anna: Well, they don't have to deal with the side effects, do they? I don't even know if I'll keep taking this medication.

Here's what it would sound like if the other person's feelings and experiences (not necessarily their beliefs) are validated:

Anna: I hate this medication for my diabetes. I wish I didn't have to take it.

Jane: What's the worst part about it?

Anna: It makes me tired and nauseous and I don't think it's even helping.

Jane: I can understand why you don't like it. It must be hard to keep taking it.

Anna: Yeah, but I need to take it. Otherwise my diabetes will be out of control.

Ironically, by validating others rather than trying to convince them something's not that bad, we're more likely to actually make them feel better. This is what it means to get in the boat with someone; you validate your friend's experience so she knows she's not alone in whatever she's feeling. Notice that this doesn't involve having to validate that someone's beliefs are correct (for example, Jane didn't have to say, "You're right, the medication isn't working"), just the person's feelings (for example, "I can understand why you don't like it").

Research has shown the importance of having others in our boat with us. In one study, researchers had participants stand at the bottom of a hill and estimate how tall it was

(Schnall et al. 2008). If participants stood with a loved one, they estimated the hill to be less high than when they were alone. In another study, participants estimated the weight of a backpack that they'd have to carry. If they were with a loved one—knowing full well that the other person would not help them carry the backpack—they estimated that the backpack was lighter than when they were alone. As you can see, when we have the support of others, the hills we have to climb in life seem smaller, and the weights we have to carry seem lighter.

In a series of amazing studies (Johnson et al. 2013; Coan, Schaefer, and Davidson 2006), researchers looked at the impact that having others in our boat had on our experience of pain. These researchers used functional magnetic resonance imaging (fMRI) to measure brain activity in participants whose toes were shocked. The fMRI allowed researchers to observe the experience of pain based on the brain's response. When participants held the hand of a loved one, their brain showed less pain, whereas when they were alone it showed more (the shock administered was always the same). When they were shocked alone, participants described the shock as "excruciating," but when they held the hand of a loved one they described it as "not a big deal."

It's important to note that these researchers (Johnson et al. 2013) also found that distressed relationships can make dealing with life's hurdles even more difficult—that is, "holding the hand" of this person can actually make the pain feel worse. You're better off alone than seeking support from this person in times of need. We only benefit from having someone else there if we're in a secure, stable relationship with that person.

So all of this is to say that when we have supportive, stable, loving relationships, the obstacles don't seem as big, the burdens don't seem as heavy, and the pain isn't as bad. Having someone in your boat doesn't take the pain away, but it adds comfort, which makes pain and difficulties more bearable. You will face many unsolvable problems in life and with your health; it's to your benefit to not do so alone.

Choice Point

Having read this chapter, you can add some more information to the choice point worksheet. Under "skills" you can write "assertive communication," which can help you with your healthy habits. Under "passengers that get in the way" you can write down some of your maladaptive interpersonal styles, such as pleasing people or passiveness, which can get in the way of your healthy habits. For example, I often need to be assertive and ask for my needs to be met in order to get to the gym, because I often need the help of others, whether that's getting someone else to watch my kid or telling my kid that I'm going to miss his sports practice. My passengers will say things like "Don't be difficult," or "Don't bother others with requests," or "Your son will be upset." But I need to go to the gym anyway, despite the discomfort I might feel. It helps to remind myself of the rumble strip I have to go over in order to be assertive.

Remember, the part that you control is you. This means that your job is to ask assertively, and to try to get in the boat with your loved ones. These behaviors increase the likelihood that you'll receive the same treatment from others in your life, even though you don't control them.

CHAPTER 8

You Will Fall off the Wagon

Maintaining a healthy habit is very challenging. Life is going to get in your way. Maybe you get sick or your kid gets sick and you stop going to the gym, or you end up at a holiday party face-to-face with your favorite treats and end up eating way too much. It's not a question of if you will fall off the wagon—that is, stop engaging in your healthy habits—it's a question of how quickly can you get back on. You will fall off the wagon, because you're only human, but do you get back on the next morning, next Monday, or a year from now?

Most people engage in some all-or-nothing thinking when they fall off the wagon: *Well, I blew it, I might as well just eat whatever I want.* With this kind of thinking, small lapses can turn into long relapses, during which we can undo a lot of the positive effects of our efforts, so it's key to get back to your healthy habit as quickly as possible. In this chapter we're going to look at how long it takes to establish healthy habits, what you can do when you fall off the wagon, and, of course, the passengers who might get in the way of sticking to them.

The "Twenty-One Days to Build a Habit" Myth

Perhaps you've heard that it takes twenty-one days to build a habit. Unfortunately there is no scientific evidence to back this up (Clear 2014). It actually takes more like two to three years to build a healthy habit. Yes, this probably is discouraging to hear, but I share it in the hopes that you'll be more compassionate with yourself if you try a health behavior for twenty-one days and it doesn't stick. You're not a failure, it just takes longer than this to establish a habit.

It takes at least one calendar year of persistence and consistency for you to figure out how to keep a habit going. After a year you've been tested by typical events, such as Thanksgiving and Christmas and the like. The second year through you're a bit wiser; you're a bit better at sticking with your habit. But sometimes it takes until the third year for you to notice the absence of your healthy habit, and this will somehow feel odd and remind you to reengage in it. Healthy habits don't ever become automatic, but they can become part of your routine so that you notice your effort less often. It's helpful to remind yourself of these facts when you struggle to maintain healthy habits or fall off the wagon altogether. If you're kind with yourself, it's less likely that a lapse will turn into a long-term relapse.

Chutes and Ladders

In the board game Chutes and Ladders (or Snakes and Ladders), you roll dice and move your piece along squares on the board accordingly. If you land on a square with a chute, you have to slide down the chute to a lower square. If you land on a square with a ladder, you get to climb the ladder, skipping a bunch of squares and moving into a winning position faster. The first player to get to the top square wins.

Our efforts to stick to healthy habits can be a lot like Chutes and Ladders. There will be times when you stop doing your healthy habit and it feels like you have to start at the beginning again. This is like hitting a chute and sliding back to an earlier square. But the more you work on getting back to doing your healthy habit, the more often you will hit ladders. That is to say, you will get back to where you were faster than the first time you had to get back to your healthy habit.

Here's a concrete example. When I was trying to establish a regular habit of exercise, I caught a cold and stopped going to the gym. This was like hitting a chute. It was a month before I got back to the gym. When I started going again, it felt like starting over. I was sore after workouts and it felt really hard to get back at it. But I kept at it. The next time I stopped going to the gym it only took two weeks to get back to going again instead of four weeks. I had hit a ladder. I got back to where

I had been with my fitness faster than after the first time I stopped going to the gym. If you keep at it, it will get easier to get back to your healthy habit each time you stop engaging in it. You will hit more ladders and get back to where you were faster.

What to Do When You Fall Off the Wagon

Responding to ourselves with self-compassion when we fall off the wagon is an effective way to get back on the wagon. Although it's a common cultural belief that being hard on ourselves can motivate us, the research doesn't support this idea. While being hard on yourself can *sometimes* help you get started with a new behavior, it rarely helps you keep it up, and often it can undermine your efforts. In contrast, research has shown that being kind to yourself in the face of setbacks can help you persist at difficult tasks (Hope, Koestner, and Milyavskaya 2014; Neely et al. 2009).

After falling off the wagon, many people decide to get back to it by doing *all* their health behaviors at once. My client, John, had fallen off the wagon and was determined to get back on it full force: "I've got to start counting my calories and get back to walking every day and start measuring my portions and start bringing my lunch to work every day." Does that sound daunting and overwhelming? Of course it does! And if you've attempted to get back on the wagon in this manner, you've probably struggled. The trick to getting back to your health behaviors more quickly is to ease yourself back onto the wagon so it's not such a punishing task.

Before you fall off the wagon (that is, right now), identify the simplest, easiest SMART goal related to your healthy habit (see chapter 3) that you can reach for that would symbolize getting back on the wagon. Think about adding or doing things (for example, eating more vegetables, drinking a glass of water, or going for a ten-minute walk) instead of not doing things or taking things away (for example, don't eat fast food, stop eating chocolate). Here are some steps you can take to get back on the wagon in a compassionate way:

1. Notice what happened. (For example, "I was trying to watch my portions but I ended up at a buffet and ate until I was stuffed.")

2. Notice how your self-critical passenger will judge you automatically. (For example, *Why did I do that? What's the matter with me? I can't believe I undid all my hard work. This is never going to work!*)

3. Respond to that judgment with curiosity and an observer perspective. (For example, "Wow! Look at how my mind is judging me. It's sure working hard to try to motivate me.")

4. Recognize that whatever choice you made, you were likely acting just like a human being is supposed to. (For example, "My body and mind have evolved to prefer sugary, fatty, salty foods and to eat as much as possible whenever it's available, so eating everything at the buffet is exactly

what my body has evolved to do.")

5. Congratulate yourself. (For example, "Congrats! I am a well-functioning human.")

6. Remind yourself that almost everyone else has done the same thing. (For example, "We've all overeaten.")

7. Give yourself a hug, tell yourself something kind, and imagine what your compassionate passenger might say. (For example, "You're a human like everyone else, and we all make mistakes. Just get back on the wagon.")

8. Use the SMART goal you've already identified to get back on track. Try to get back to your behavior as soon as possible: before you finish the bag of chips, after dinner, or before bed. Don't wait until tomorrow morning, next Monday, or January 1.

9. With kindness and self-compassion ease yourself back onto the wagon with your easy, healthy SMART goal that you identified ahead of time. Congratulate yourself for

being a well-functioning human who can respond to yourself with kindness in the face of setbacks and personal failings.

Passenger Tricks

After you've fallen off the wagon it can be useful to review what your passengers did to help knock you off your route, what "passenger tricks" they used. Did they convince you that you couldn't do some behavior or that you shouldn't, or did they put you on automatic pilot? Some of my personal favorites (that is, the ones my passengers love telling me) are "There's ice cream. You love ice cream! It's your favorite!" Or "You've had such a long hard day. You deserve a treat." Or "You don't have time for that."

As I mentioned already, your passengers aren't out to get you, nor are they trying to harm you—quite the opposite. They are doing their best to take care of you. And if you were a cave person, their suggestions would likely be very helpful for short-term survival. But because we live in modern times, there's a good chance that their suggestions will lead you away from your values and healthy habits. Falling for passenger tricks with regularity won't help you stick to your healthy habits in the long term.

The first step to overcoming passenger tricks is to recognize that they are never going away. Once your mind finds what it thinks is a survival strategy, it will never let go of it. And, of course, this is very appropriate in an evolutionary context. Remember that cave person from earlier in the book who survived a bear attack but then forgot all about it. He is not our ancestor. A well-functioning mind, one equipped for survival, would remember this bear attack and remind the survivor of it whenever possible. Even if this person moved to the Sahara Desert, where bears don't live, he'd still remember the bear attack. This is how the mind works.

So, you can't rid yourself of passenger tricks, but you can develop skills so you are less likely to fall for them. Think of it this way: Like most people, you probably receive spam in your inbox either warning you of something terrible ("Your accounts have been frozen") or exciting ("You're the winner of a huge jackpot"), and all you have to do is click on the link to fix your account or collect your prize. If you've ever clicked one of these links, you likely opened a virus that wreaked havoc on your computer. We can't stop the spam from arriving, but we can stop ourselves from clicking the link, and the same is true of our passengers. We can't stop the passengers from offering the tricks, but we don't have to fall for them. I touched on some of these tricks in previous chapters, but we're going to review a few more and look at ways to deal with them.

Why?

"Why" questions—Why can't I control my eating? Why do I have such a bad relationship with food? Why can't I quit smoking? Why do I hate exercise so much?—all result in the same thing: an exploration for the underlying reasons *why* you are behaving the way you are behaving. This type of questioning is very normal. It's part of our default problem-solving brain. And it's very effective for solving problems in the external environment. For example, asking yourself why your shelter keeps falling apart increases the likelihood that you'll figure out how to fix it. However, this same "why" questioning is typically not as effective for addressing our own behavior.

Here's an example of the problem with spending too much time focusing on the "why." During most of our sessions Wendy constantly wanted to try to get to the bottom of why she turned to drinking when she was stressed. The first problem with this type of thinking is that there are a huge number of factors that influence our behavior. Here are just a few of the factors that impacted Wendy's use of alcohol in response to stress: her physiological response to alcohol, her expectations about the calming effects of drinking, having seen her parents have cocktail hour after a long day at work, her circle of friends who always had a drink at social functions. The human mind is incapable of pinpointing all the factors that influence our behavior and their relative contributions to our behavior. The second problem is that even if we could somehow figure out what caused her relationship with alcohol, what then? Could Wendy do anything about her parents' cocktail hour or about her physiological response to alcohol? No! There is no "fixing" these contributions to the problem the way we can "fix" the factors contributing to our shelter falling down.

So trying to figure out why you behave a certain way is a trick of the mind, of your passengers. You'll waste incredible amounts of time with very few results for your efforts. Thus, rather than focusing on the "why," focus on what the passengers tell you in the here and now that leads you to drink (or smoke or eat too much or skip the gym). Focusing on how the passengers knock you off course in the here and now is more likely to change your behavior than understanding "why" you behave that way.

I Deserve a Break

I've had a hard day. I deserve a break. Ever had a thought like that? Isn't it interesting that our passengers never seem to say, "You should treat yourself with some healthy broccoli." Nope. If your mind is like most minds, it will suggest drinking or smoking or avoiding the gym or consuming some sugary, salty, fatty food.

Our passengers' suggestion for an unhealthy break is all about a short-term fix, not the long-term consequences. No surprises here, as our brain evolved to be very focused on surviving in the now with little thought of the future. I'm not going to try to convince you that you don't deserve a break. You do! I just want you to learn to notice when your passengers are suggesting a short-term fix to how you're feeling, and that these can lead to long-term harm.

Below are some alternative ways to take a break that engage at least one of the five senses. Keep in mind that none of these options will be as effective at answering your passengers as eating or smoking or drinking, because you're hardwired to respond positively to these actions. Taking a relaxing bath will never be as easy or enjoyable as eating a chocolate bar on the way home from work, so be mindful of your expectations. But also remember that these alternative breaks won't cost you much in the long run.

Touch
Caress a silk scarf or a fleece blanket.
Place a warm or cold washcloth on your face.
Cocoon yourself in a blanket.
Wear your favorite outfit.
Take a relaxing bath.

Sight
Watch your favorite movie.
Look at a sentimental object (jewelry, pictures).
Look at beautiful pictures.

Hearing
Listen to a water fountain.
Play your favorite music.

Smell

Light a candle.
Try aromatherapy.

Taste
Sip hot or cold tea.
Chew gum.
Suck on a mint.

If it doesn't seem like any of these options might work, you can come up with your own, or you can try bringing to mind your compassionate figure. Imagine how she might comfort you. Think about her sitting beside you, maybe putting her arm around you and saying something comforting, like "It's going to be okay." Lastly, spend some money if you need to: buy a trashy magazine, new makeup, or a woodworking tool, or get your nails done or have a massage. If doing this feels too luxurious, remind yourself that you would have spent money on food or alcohol or cigarettes anyway, so it's okay to spend money to avoid using these unhealthy habits as a treat. However, I leave you with this caveat: be mindful of not overdoing it, as "retail therapy" (feeling good through shopping) can also have some long-term negative consequences.

She's Naturally That Way

One of my friends from my kid's school is very thin. She has four children and is probably a size zero. When she walks in a room, one of the other mothers who's present invariably says something like "How does she look like that?" And someone will answer, "Oh, she's just naturally that way." As our friendship developed, I realized there was much more to the picture than this oft-repeated refrain. For example, she once told me about a power outage that had occurred at her house, during which the power was only on for an hour in a twenty-four hour period. Guess what she did for that one hour. Do you think she prioritized what I normally do in such a situation? Charging my cell phone, downloading videos to watch offline, making some food ... Wrong! She ran on her treadmill.

And then there was the night I went out to dinner with this same mom and some other friends. After about an hour I realized we had only talked about weight-management strategies the whole time: "What do you eat for breakfast?" "What kind of protein powder do you like best?" "What's the healthiest drink to have at a restaurant?" This is not my typical conversation when I go out for supper. This mom also had a long conversation with the waitress about the healthiest food option on the menu, and she ended up ordering a salad. I'm pretty sure I had a burger and fries. So contrary to the myth that some people are just "naturally that way," most of us, including this mom, have to work hard at it.

Convincing you that everyone else has it easy and it's just you who has to work at a particular behavior is an old passenger trick. This line of thinking usually ends with a "Why bother?" and a justification for you to move away from your healthy habits. It's true, there are people who are naturally a size zero (or who quit smoking the first try or who run a 10K race without training), but they are the exception, not the rule.

Apparently even Gisele Bündchen follows a sugar-free, plant-based diet.

But My Values Conflict

Clients often perceive that there's a conflict between engaging in healthy habits and being an engaged parent, both of which are values. One of my clients had diabetes and had to monitor his blood sugar during the day. He found this disruptive because he couldn't participate continuously in family events. So one of his passengers convinced him that his values were in conflict, and he needed to choose between the two.

I asked him why managing his blood sugar was important? "So I can stay healthy," he said. Why did he want to stay healthy? "So I can be around for my daughter." Thus, we uncovered that his values were not in conflict, rather they went together. Managing his blood sugar was just another way to express his value of being an engaged parent. If you have a passenger telling you your values conflict, explore them more deeply. Sometimes what seems like a conflicting value is just a different way of expressing the same value. For example, healthy habits can be your way of expressing being an engaged parent.

I Might as Well Give In

We all face different kinds of urges or cravings. They might be for food or to spend money shopping or to drink or to smoke. And most of us worry that these urges or cravings will go on forever, increasing in intensity unless we give in to them. In fact, our passengers may convince us that the only way to manage them is to give in to them. This is another trick. Urges or cravings are actually more like waves. They will rise, peak, and then dissipate just as ocean waves do on the beach. So I invite you to try this next exercise, imagining that your urge or craving is like a wave, and you are a surfer (inspired by Lillis, Dahl, and Weineland 2014).

First, think of an urge or craving you have. Imagine the food, or drink, or cigarette that prompts that craving until you notice it showing up in you. Can you explore this urge or craving like a curious scientist, as if you've never encountered it before? What does it feel like? Where do you feel it most intensely in your body? What thoughts or feelings come up? Can you notice these with nonjudgmental curiosity?

This urge or craving is part of being a human. It exists because you are a well-functioning human. See if you can imagine dropping the struggle with the urge or craving? Can you imagine making space for these sensations with curiosity and kindness? We are used to just giving in to cravings, so see if you can stick with the feelings with willingness and openness without having to make them go away.

Now, imagine that this urge or craving is like a wave, and you're riding this wave with your breath. Notice the sensations of the urge or craving as they rise and eventually peak. With each breath make space for these sensations.

With each breath notice the sensations with willingness. Imagine that with each breath you can surf this wave of craving and you can ride it to the shore as it crests and dissipates on the beach.

With practice you can develop the skill of surfing your urges or cravings. In order to improve this skill, you need to encounter urges or cravings without giving in to them, so it's best to practice with your easiest urges or cravings first, working your way up to the hardest ones. So if drinking beer is a craving of yours, don't try to surf your cravings for beer (rather than giving in to your craving and drinking beer) when you're at a bar surrounded by beer. Try something easier first; try surfing the craving by imagining a beer. Once you're good at surfing your cravings for beer while imagining beer, then you can move on to more difficult situations (such as when there is an actual beer nearby). Notice that I'm suggesting that you should get to know your cravings better rather than avoiding them. Willingness to experience cravings is a big part of creating a different relationship with them.

I Hate Exercise

One of my clients started exercising at the gym as an expression of her value of creativity. That is, she recognized that exercising at the gym left her calmer, in a better mood, and consequently more creative. "How is the exercise going?" I asked her during one of our sessions. "Awful," she said, "I hate exercise. I'm just not an exercise person." I decided to probe this line of thinking with a few questions: What did she notice before she went to the gym? What did she notice while exercising? Before she went she felt mostly dread, and while at the gym she felt pretty uncomfortable. These answers seemed to correlate with her hatred of exercise, so I then asked her what she felt *after* she exercised. She said that she noticed a feeling of pride. Before this inquiry she hadn't noticed this feeling because her passengers had hijacked the story of her exercise. They had convinced her that the whole thing was awful and glossed over the pride aspect.

We can get caught up in old stories—"I'm not that kind of person," "I hate exercise," and so on—that describe an experience quite differently from what we actually experienced from moment to moment. Just as my client only remembered what she hated about exercise, you, too, may be overlooking positive aspects of some experience of yours. Try using present-moment awareness to observe what you experience before, during, and after you engage in certain health behaviors. Remember, it's quite likely that the before and the during may not be pleasant (avoiding the gym is more likely to feel good in the short term than is having for a hard workout). It's the after where you'll notice the biggest difference (if you avoid the gym you're likely to feel guilty, disappointed, or angry with yourself, whereas if you go to the gym you're likely to feel proud and capable). You may discover that your passengers are hijacking your experiences. (The "Value-Consistent Behavior" worksheet, available at http:

//www.newharbinger.com/43317, can help you explore this further.)

Don't Fall for It

When I try to put my eight-year-old son to bed, right when I'm about to turn off the lights, he often says, "I have to go to the bathroom," or "I need some water," or "I'm hungry." Over time I learned to make sure that he goes to the bathroom, has a drink of water, and has some food before we start the bedtime routine. Now when he says these things I know he's just trying to get out of going to bed. I can say to him, "Oh, I know this trick, and I'm not falling for it." And then I tell him I love him and I'll see him when he wakes up. And I turn off the lights.

You'll never be able to stop your passengers from trying to trick you. Your job, as it was for me with my son, is to notice their tricks and to not fall for them.

Choice Point

Having read this chapter, you can add more information to the choice point worksheet. You can write down several of the common tricks passengers play on us under "passengers that get in the way." Pick the ones that are more common or convincing for you (for example, "I deserve a break"). You can also add several skills related to getting back on the wagon (being kind to yourself, easing yourself back onto the wagon, identifying a SMART goal related to your healthy habits) and ways to not fall for passenger tricks (for example, thanking passengers or reminding yourself to "not click the spam link"). For example, when I'm trying to get to the gym my passengers often try to trick me with the "But it's true" trick (usually related to the thought *I'm too tired to go to the gym*). So that's something I could write under "passengers that get in the way." I use the skill of reminding myself that it's a trick and I shouldn't fall for it, and I go to the gym anyway. I could include this under "skills."

CHAPTER 9

How Doctors Choose to Die

When faced with a terminal illness, many doctors don't choose all the life-prolonging treatments they often so readily offer their patients (White 2014). Instead they often choose to go home to die surrounded by family. This suggests that when they're faced with a terminal illness, many doctors choose quality of life over quantity. Ironically, many do the opposite for their patients, offering them quantity of life sometimes over quality of life.

The health care system is designed to prolong life, not to ensure better quality of life. It's well designed for acute illness and injury, and health care providers are taught to fix problems. With all the best intentions, many get caught up in the urge to fix patients. A physician once recounted to me the story of a patient asking if she was going to die. No, was his quick response, because he was trying to reassure her. And yet his response was entirely false. We are *all going to die.* Like many health care providers, many physicians are not well equipped to support quality-of-life choices over quantity. In general, the main goal of the health care system is to keep people alive, regardless of quality.

I remember doing an assessment with a woman who was considering a liver transplant. She had end-stage liver disease, meaning that without an intervention she would die. During the assessment she expressed ambivalence about undergoing a transplant, instead talking about wanting to just spend time with her grandchildren rather than undergoing major surgery. I remember being horrified. *This poor woman, she doesn't understand that she needs to undergo this transplant to live a longer life.* I tried to convince her to pursue a transplant. My efforts, and likely the efforts of the other transplant team members, scared her enough to convince her to undergo the surgery. The surgery itself went fine, but her recovery was far from ideal. She spent most of the following year in the hospital, where she died roughly one year after her surgery, surrounded by machines, not her family. I don't think she spent more than five days at home, and she certainly didn't spend meaningful time with her grandchildren. This case had a big impact on me. I realized that I was caught up in the same fix-it urge that many of my colleagues were, wanting to extend life rather than considering quality of life.

I handled the next patient who was ambivalent about having a transplant differently. He told me that if I could guarantee the surgery would improve his quality of life, then he'd definitely do it. I was honest with him. I told him there was no guarantee of that, as its purpose was to extend life. I said, "Some people do recover and have better quality of life, but not everyone. It's okay if you don't want the surgery. It's okay if you decide you just want go home and spend the time you have left with your family." He left the hospital a few days later, and after a few weeks he died at home.

I had a colleague who was asked to speak to a patient who had just had her second leg amputation because of complications with diabetes. Much to the horror of her doctors this patient was still smoking, and my colleague's task was to try to get her to stop smoking. My colleague gave her the spiel about how detrimental smoking was, especially for people with diabetes. The patient responded, "Look, I know I'm not gonna live a long life. Smoking is the last thing that's enjoyable in my life." My colleague looked at her and said, "I hear ya. Go enjoy your life." There's no debate about whether smoking is bad for your health. It clearly is. But my colleague recognized that the patient was choosing quality of life over quantity.

I've spent most of the book trying to help you live a healthier life. But here's the thing: it doesn't really matter to me if this book made you healthier. What matters to me is that being healthier has helped you live a more meaningful, purposeful, vibrant life. My question is not do you want to live longer, it's what are you going to do with your extra years of life? From my perspective, any effort put toward being healthier is meant to be in service of your values, of living a life that matters to you.

When we hit holiday time at the obesity clinic, clients would say that they were just going to skip holiday parties that year in order to manage their weight. Sure, that's definitely a strategy to employ, but at what cost? You might end up reducing or holding your weight if you skip all social functions, but your quality of life suffers. There are many costs to choosing healthy habits, and you may decide that some are not consistent with your values. For example, when it's up to me to choose my meals, I tend to make plant-based meals. But if I get invited to someone's house for dinner, I don't tell them I need a vegan meal, and I don't bring a vegan meal with me. That's because this meal with a friend isn't just about food. It's about the host offering something they've made; it's about their efforts to plan and create a meal and to welcome and host me. So I *choose* not to disrupt those aspects by insisting on following my plant-based diet at all cost.

Best weight (Freedhoff and Sharma 2010) is a weight-management idea based on the smallest number of calories one can consume daily that still allows the person to enjoy each day. Best weight is the weight you can achieve while living the healthiest lifestyle you can truly enjoy. I think this strategy can be expanded to include all healthy habits. You don't have to pick *the* healthiest option every time (and beat yourself up if you don't). It's okay to choose something *just a little bit* healthier than what you were choosing before, and to balance healthy habits with living a life that matters.

You may be thinking that I'm suggesting that quality of life and quantity of life are opposites, and if you choose one you can't choose the other. Often our mind seems to only give us two options to choose from, either quality of life or healthy habits. This line of reasoning is similar to that passenger who tricks you into believing your values are in conflict. But there's the third option: healthy habits do contribute to quality of life.

I went to a conference where Dr. Kenneth Rockwood, an expert on aging and frailty, discussed the impact of healthy habits on life span (Rockwood 2017). He showed a picture of a ninety-year-old man running a marathon and said this man had died shortly after the picture was taken. He explained that healthy living doesn't just extend your number of years on Earth, it also extends the number of *quality* years you have on Earth. He pointed out that a rapid decline at the end of one's life is actually the ideal scenario. This marathon runner had spent most of his life being able to do the things that mattered to him. He had a rapid decline near the end and spent only a few days in the hospital before passing away. Thus, he only spent a small part of his life having a low quality of life—and this was the effect of his healthy habits.

A New Stick to Beat You With?

I had a client who told me she was really put together. She had a good job that she was good at, and she had good friends and a great family. What she couldn't figure out was why she couldn't manage her eating and her weight. She burst into tears as she wondered out loud, "Why can't I get control over this? I should be able to control my eating! I should be able to manage this!" This is a familiar tale.

Many people who are incredibly successful in most aspects of their life struggle to "control" their healthy habits, and there are many reasons why this is so common. First, smoking, drinking, and sleeping instead of going to the gym are all preferences of your cave person brain. Remember the cave person who chose to rest rather than go for a run, and thus he had the energy to outrun a predator? His choices were beneficial as a cave person but aren't necessarily the healthy ones in our modern world. When it comes to eating and weight, there are layers of systems in the brain and body that ensure we don't starve to death (chapter 1), and these systems are difficult to "control." The moment you stop engaging your frontal lobe, your cave person brain will take over, and you'll do things consistent with avoiding starving to death (for example, eating when you're not hungry; eating until the plate is empty; choosing foods high in sugar, salt, and fat). Remember that almost any healthy habit is going to violate the principles of your caveperson brain—that is, your hardwiring!

Second, our environment, especially in developed Western nations, is full of triggers for unhealthy habits—especially those related to food. Driving down the street you're bombarded with fastfood restaurants and billboards showing foods of every stripe. Practically every commercial on TV sends you signals to eat. Office, school, and social functions are full of the unhealthiest food. Your kids' sporting events include deep-fried options, rarely vegetables. This extends to most other healthy habits. We have all kinds of machines that reduce our physical activity: cars, washing machines, grocery stores. Most of us have jobs that are sedentary. Alcohol and cigarettes have been adapted by industries to make us like them more. Although you may be very capable of controlling yourself in many areas of life, it shouldn't surprise you that sticking to any healthy habit is much more difficult.

Third, many "successful" people have used problem-focused coping (chapter 7) to great results in life, rarely needing to use emotion-focused coping. The long-term management of health, however, requires emotion-focused coping, because many aspects of health don't have a "fix." For example, quitting smoking requires us to manage cravings on an ongoing basis (no fix). Exercise is only effective when we do it regularly, so we have to keep exercising for it to impact our health (once again, no fix). So if you've been successful as a result of using problem-focused coping most of your life, it makes sense that you'd lack the emotion-focused coping strategies needed to manage long-term health. You haven't needed them to be successful.

And, fourth, there are all the factors we went over in chapter 2 that you have little control over and yet influence your struggle with weight or sticking to healthy habits. How many of them seemed relevant to your struggles? Did you choose your parents or your ancestors? Did you choose your genetics or to be born in a Western culture inundated with unhealthy triggers, including those related to food? Did you choose to have a cave person brain focused on survival? No! Of course you didn't, but they affect you nonetheless.

Reviewing this information with clients is meant to induce self-compassion, showing them some of the roadblocks to healthy living. I've noticed that some of my clients' passengers hijack this info and use it against them instead. The same "put-together" client who cried about not being able to control her eating was one of these. Knowing about the evolutionary and cultural reasons why she struggled to control her eating made her feel worse. Why? Because now she *really knew better,* and she'd been taught all sorts of skills from an expert (me, apparently), and she still couldn't eat healthy all the time. Basically her self-critical passenger found a new stick to beat her with.

This book is not meant to be a new stick to beat yourself with. Just because you've read it and (hopefully) gained a new perspective and learned some new skills doesn't mean that you now are going to be able to "control" your healthy habits permanently. This will always require effort. I have no expectation that going forward you'll always choose the healthy option. In fact, I'm giving you permission to choose an unhealthy option—just do so because it's a deliberate choice and not because your passengers have hijacked your bus. It all comes down to personal choice and what quality of life you're comfortable with. I find the "description, prediction, choice" model (Vallis 2015) useful for creating context for some of life's choices:

> *Description:* You have diabetes, but you like to eat sweets and tend to avoid testing your blood sugar.

Prediction: There will be negative long-term consequences for your health if you don't manage your blood sugar.

Choice: Are you okay with that?

It's okay to say, "Yes, right now I'm going to pick the short-term benefit." Remember, the content of this entire book is in the service of you leading a vibrant, meaningful life, not just to make you skinnier, or have lower cholesterol, or eat healthier, or stop smoking.

Keeping It Going

This book has been about sticking to healthy habits in the long term. By now your choice point worksheet should include a lot of information that you can use to help you stick with your healthy habit, including the values you identified, your SMART goal to help you express your values, the different passengers (for example, thoughts, feelings, sensations, memories, cravings, and tricks) that might get in your way, as well as a range of skills, including mindfulness, present-moment awareness, self-compassion, taking care of feelings, and so forth.

Let's review the worksheet using my illustrative example of "exercise more." I've now clarified my values about this goal (to be strong) and turned it into a SMART goal (exercise two times per week for twenty minutes). I've pinpointed the most common passengers that get in my way, including thoughts like *I don't have time for that* or feeling tired. I've recognized that my self-critical passenger is likely to criticize me ("It's never going to work") and make me feel even less motivated to go the gym. I've also documented some of the skills that work best for me to keep me moving toward what matters. Thanking passengers, compassionate hands, putting down the football, and present-moment awareness are the ones that I use most often to help me stick with my healthy habit. So now when a passenger—for example, "I don't have time for that"—shows up, I can notice it and make a choice about whether to move toward or away from what matters to me. Rather than acting automatically and doing what my passengers are telling me to, I have created a moment of choice. Do I want to follow my "I don't have time for that" passenger (which will move me away from my values), or do I want to try to move toward my values? This is my choice point. I use various skills (for example, thanking the passengers) to try to move myself just a bit more toward sticking to my healthy habit.

Hopefully by making use of the choice point worksheet and all the skills from this book you can give yourself more choice points—that is, more moments when you can consciously decide to stick to your healthy habit. Healthy living requires effort and a willingness to do the hard work of managing behaviors, even when you don't want to.

Conclusion

A year has passed since I started writing this book. I still haven't lost all my "divorce weight." Yes, I'm sure you were hoping that at the end I would finally give you the magic secret to losing weight, or to quitting smoking, or to exercising more. Sorry! Am I healthier? Hell, yeah. I now work out regularly five to six times a week. It took me three years to get into the habit of going to boot camp three times a week. Now when I don't go I feel a bit odd. Even still, when the alarm goes off at 5:30a.m., I still think *I don't want to go to boot camp. I wish I could stay in bed.* And while I'm at boot camp I curse my trainers most of the time. (Love you, Mitch and Matt! See https:/ /evolvefitnessltd.fitproconnect.com/trans formationcanada.) I remind myself often that it's my job to do my health behaviors; what my body does with them isn't up to me. There are still many parts of my body that make me cringe. But I really love what my body can do. It will dance when I want to dance. It will climb when I want to climb. And it will run when I want to run. So I'm grateful to my body for the things I can do, for the ways in which my body and my health help me live the life that really matters to me.

So as you embark on this lifelong journey, I don't wish for you to be happy or to have high self-esteem. As we've already discussed, happiness and self-esteem are unhelpful life goals. I do hope you have opportunities for joy. I hope you are as healthy as you can be. I hope your health helps you live a vibrant, purposeful, and meaningful life that really matters to you. I hope you are kind to yourself for all the ways you will fall off the wagon. (Congrats, you're human!) I hope when you get to the end of your life you look back and think, *Damn, I lived a good life.* So thank you for spending time with me and this book. I thank you and all your passengers for being with me. May you be well.

Acknowledgments

Thank you to my family and friends for supporting me, including my parents, my sister, and "the girls." To my son for making me want to be a better person every day. To all my mentors and teachers for helping me grow. To the ACBS community for being the most welcoming and supportive professional community I've ever known; you've helped me succeed in ways I never even dreamed possible.

References

Abramson, L.Y., M.E. Seligman, and J.D. Teasdale. 1978. "Learned Helplessness in Humans: Critique and Reformulation." *Journal of Abnormal Psychology* 87 (1): 49–74.

American Heart Association. 2014. *Heart Disease and Stroke Statistics—At-a-Glance.* December 17. https://www.heart.org/idc/groups/aham ah-public/@wcm/@sop/@smd/documen ts/downloadable/ucm_470704.pdf.

Bartle, N.C. 2012. "Is Social Clustering of Obesity Due to Social Contagion or Genetic Transmission?" *American Journal of Public Health* 102 (1): 7.

Bowen, S., N. Chawla, and G.A. Marlatt. 2011. *Mindfulness-Based Relapse Prevention for Addictive Behaviors: A Clinician's Guide.* New York: Guilford Press.

Bowlby, J. 1969. *Attachment and Loss.* Vol.1: Attachment. New York: Basic Books.

Bowlby, J. 1973. *Attachment and Loss.* Vol.2: Separation, Anxiety, and Anger. New York: Basic Books.

Cappuccio, F.P., F.M. Taggart, N.B. Kandala, A. Currie, E. Peile, S. Stranges, and M.A. Miller. 2008. "Meta-Analysis of Short Sleep Duration and Obesity in Children and Adults." *Sleep* 31 (5): 619–626.

Carmichael, C.L., H.T. Reis, and P.R. Duberstein. 2015. "In Your 20s It's Quantity, In Your 30s It's Quality: The Prognostic Value of Social Activity Across 30 Years of Adulthood." *Psychology and Aging* 30 (1): 95–105.

Carver, C.S., M.F. Scheier, and J.K. Weintraub. 1989. "Assessing Coping Strategies: A Theoretically Based Approach." *Journal of Personality and Social Psychology* 56 (2): 267–283.

Centers for Disease Control and Prevention. 2018. "Adult Obesity Facts." Last updated August 13. https://www.cdc.gov/obesity/data/adult.html.

Chaput, J.P., Z.M. Ferraro, D. Prud'homme, and A.M. Sharma. 2014. "Widespread Misconceptions About Obesity." *Canadian Family Physician* 60 (11): 973–975.

Christakis, N.A., and J.H. Fowler. 2007. "The Spread of Obesity in a Large Social Network over 32 Years." *New England Journal Of Medicine* 357 (4): 370–379.

Ciarrochi, J., A. Bailey, and R. Harris. 2013. *The Weight Escape: How to Stop Dieting and Start Living.* Boston: Shambhala.

Clear, J. 2014. "How Long Does It Actually Take to Form a New Habit? (Backed by Science). Huffington Post. April 10. https://www.huffingtonpost.com/james-clear/forming-new-habits_b_5104807.html.

Coan, J.A., H.S. Schaefer, and R.J. Davidson. 2006. "Lending a Hand: Social Regulation of the Neural Response to Threat." *Psychological Science* 17 (12): 1032–1039.

Coughlin, J.W., P.J. Brantley, C.M. Champagne, W.M. Vollmer, V.J. Stevens, K. Funk, A.T. Dalcin, G.J. Jerome, V.H. Myers, C. Tyson, B.C. Batch, J. Charleston, C.M. Loria, A. Bauck, J.F. Hollis, L.P. Svetkey, and L.J. Appel; Weight Loss Maintenance Collaborative Research Group. 2016. "The Impact of Continued Intervention on Weight: Five-Year Results from the Weight Loss Maintenance Trial." *Obesity* 24 (5): 1046–1053.

Cozolino, L.J. 2010. *The Neuroscience of Psychotherapy: Healing the Social Brain.* 2nd ed. New York: W.W. Norton.

Dahl, J. and T. Lundgren. 2006. *Living Beyond Your Pain: Using Acceptance and Commitment Therapy to Ease Chronic Pain.* Oakland, CA: New Harbinger.

Day, A., and D. Lee-Baggley. 2017. *ACTion: Awareness and Commitment Training in Organizations and Networks. Participant Manual.* Halifax, NS: Day and Lee-Baggley.

Depue, R.A., and J.V. Morrone-Strupinsky. 2005. "A Neuro behavioral Model of Affiliative Bonding: Implications for Conceptualizing a Human Trait of Affiliation." *Behavioral and Brain Sciences* 28 (3): 313–395.

Dulloo, A.G., J. Jacquet, and L. Girardier. 1996. "Autoregulation of Body Composition During Weight Recovery in Human: The Minnesota Experiment Revisited." *International Journal of Obesity* 20 (5): 393–405.

Eisenberger, N.I., M.D. Lieberman, and K.D. Williams. 2003. "Does Rejection Hurt? An fMRI Study of Social Exclusion." *Science* 302 (5643): 290–292.

Flaxman, P.E., F.W. Bond, and F. Livhelm. 2013. *The Mindful and Effective Employee: An Acceptance and*

Commitment Therapy Training Manual for Improving Well-Being and Performance. Oakland, CA: New Harbinger.

Fothergill, E., J. Guo, L. Howard, J.C. Kerns, N.D. Knuth, R. Brychta, K.Y. Chen, M.C. Skarulis, M. Walter, P.J. Walter, and K.D. Hall. 2016. "Persistent Metabolic Adaptation 6 Years After 'The Biggest Loser' Competition." *Obesity (Silver Spring)* 24 (8): 1612–1619.

Freedhoff, Y., and A.M. Sharma. 2010. *Best Weight: A Practical Guide to Office-Based Obesity Management.* Edmonton, AB: Canadian Obesity Network.

Gangwisch, J.E., D. Malaspina, B. Boden-Albala, and S.B. Heymsfield. 2005. "Inadequate Sleep as a Risk Factor for Obesity: Analyses of the NHANES I." *Sleep* 28 (10): 1289–1296.

Gilbert, P. 2009a. *The Compassionate Mind: A New Approach to Life's Challenges.* London: Constable and Robinson

Gilbert, P. 2009b. "Introducing Compassion-Focused Therapy." *Advances in Psychiatric Treatment* 15 (3): 199–208.

Gilbert, P., D. Tirch, and L. Silberstein. 2017. "An Introduction to Compassion Focused Therapy." Workshop presentation at the Association for Contextual Behavioral Science World Conference 15, Seville, Spain, June 20–25, 2017.

Hafekost, K., D. Lawrence, F. Mitrou, T. A O'Sullivan, and S.R. Zubrick. 2013. "Tackling Overweight and Obesity: Does the Public Health Message Match the Science?" *BMC Medicine* 11: 41.

Hall, K.L., and J.S. Rossi. 2008. "Meta-Analytic Examination of the Strong and Weak Principles Across 48 Health Behaviors." *Preventative Medicine* 46 (3): 266–274.

Harris, R. 2008. *The Happiness Trap: How to Stop Struggling and Start Living.* Boston: Trumpeter.

Harris, R. 2009. *ACT Made Simple: An Easy-to-Read Primer on Acceptance and Commitment Therapy.* Oakland, CA: New Harbinger.

Hayes, S.C. 2005. *Get Out of Your Mind and Into Your Life: The New Acceptance and Commitment Therapy.* Oakland, CA: New Harbinger.

Hayes, S.C., K. Strosahl, and K.G. Wilson. 1999. *Acceptance and Commitment Therapy: An Experiential Approach to Behavior Change.* New York: Guilford Press.

Heart Research Institute. 2018. "Prevention." http://www.hricanada.org /prevention.

Holt-Lunstad J., T.B. Smith, and J.B. Layton. 2010. "Social Relationships and Mortality Risk: A Meta-Analytic Review." *PLoS Medicine* 7 (7): e1000316.

Hope, N., R. Koestner, and M. Milyavskaya. 2014. "The Role of Self-Compassion in Goal Pursuit and Well-Being Among University

Freshman." *Self and Identity* 13 (5): 579–593.

Hruschka, D.J., A.A. Brewis, A. Wutich, and B. Morin. 2011. "Shared Norms and Their Explanation for the Social Clustering of Obesity." *American Journal Of Public Health* 101 (Suppl 1): S295–S300.

Jackson, S.E., C. Kirschbaum, and A. Steptoe. 2017. "Hair Cortisol and Adiposity in a Population-Based Sample of 2,527 Men and Women Aged 54 to 87 Years." *Obesity (Silver Spring)* 25 (3): 539–544.

Johnson, S.M., M.B. Moser, L. Beckes, A. Smith, T. Dalgleish, R. Halchuk, K. Hasselmo, P.S. Greenman, Z. Merali, and J.A. Coan. 2013. "Soothing the Threatened Brain: Leveraging Contact Comfort with Emotionally Focused Therapy." *PLoS ONE* 8 (11): e79314.

Kabat-Zinn, J. 2016. *Mindfulness for Beginners.* Boulder, CO: Sounds True.

Kerns, J.C., J. Guo, E. Fothergill, L. Howard, N.D. Knuth, R. Brychta, K.Y. Chen, M.C. Skarulis, P.J. Walter, and K.D. Hall. 2017. "Increased Physical Activity Associated with Less Weight Regain Six Years After 'The Biggest Loser' Competition." *Obesity (Silver Spring)* 25 (11): 1838–1843.

Lillis, J., J. Dahl, and S.M. Weineland. 2014. *The Diet Trap: Feed Your Psychological Needs and End the Weight Loss Struggle Using Acceptance and Commitment Therapy.* Oakland, CA: New Harbinger.

MacBeth, A., and A. Gumley. 2012. "Exploring Compassion: A Meta-Analysis of the Association Between Self-Compassion and Psychopathology." *Clinical Psychology Review* 32: 545–552.

MacLean, P.S., A. Bergouignan, M.A. Cornier, and M.R. Jackman. 2011. "Biology's Response to Dieting: The Impetus for Weight Regain." *American Journal of Physiology: Regulatory,*

Integrative, and Comparative Physiology 301 (3): R581–R600.

Marketdata LLC. 2017. "The U.S. Weight Loss and Diet Control Market." Market research.com. May. https://www.mark etresearch.com/Marketdata-Enterprises -Inc-v416/Weight-Loss-Diet-Control-10 825677.

McGonigal, K. 2013. *The Willpower Instinct: How Self-Control Works, Why It Matters, and What You Can Do to Get More of It.* New York: Avery.

McGuire, M.T., R.R. Wing, M.L. Klem, and J.O. Hill. 1999. "Behavioral Strategies of Individuals Who Have Maintained Long-Term Weight Losses." *Obesity Research* 7 (4): 334–341.

McNeil, J., É. Doucet, and J.P. Chaput. 2013. "Inadequate Sleep as a Contributor to Obesity and Type 2 Diabetes." *Canadian Journal of Diabetes* 37 (2): 103–108.

Mikulincer, M., and P.R. Shaver. 2007a. *Attachment in Adulthood: Structure,*

Dynamics, and Change. New York: Guilford Press.

Mikulincer, M., and P.R. Shaver. 2007b. "Boosting Attachment Security to Promote Mental Health, Prosocial Values, and Inter-Group Tolerance." *Psychological Inquiry* 18 (3): 139–156.

Miyagawa, Y., and J. Taniguchi. 2016. "Development of the Japanese Version of the Self-Compassionate Reactions Inventory." *Japanese Journal of Psychology* 87 (1): 70–78.

Monèstes, J.-L., and M. Villatte. 2011. *La thérapie d'acceptation et d'engagement, ACT.* Paris: Elsevier Masson.

Muller, M.J., and A. Bosy-Westphal. 2013. "Adaptive Thermogenesis with Weight Loss in Humans." *Obesity (Silver Spring)* 21 (2): 218–228.

Neely, M.E., D.L. Schallert, S.S. Mohammed, R.M. Roberts, and Y.-J. Chen. 2009. "Self-Kindness When Facing Stress: The Role of

Self-Compassion, Goal Regulation, and Support in College Students' Well-Being." *Motivation and Emotion* 33 (1): 88–97.

Neff, K.D. 2003a. "The Development and Validation of a Scale to Measure Self-Compassion." *Self and Identity* 2 (3): 223–250.

Neff, K.D. 2003b. "Self-Compassion: An Alternative Conceptualization of a Healthy Attitude Toward Oneself." *Self and Identity* 2 (2): 85–101.

Neff, K.D. 2013. *Self-Compassion Step by Step: The Proven Power of Being Kind to Yourself.* Audio CD. Boulder, CO: Sounds True.

Neff, K.D., Y.-P. Hsieh, and K. Dejitterat. 2005. "Self-Compassion, Achievement Goals, and Coping with Academic Failure." *Self And Identity* 4 (3): 263–287.

Neff, K.D., S.S. Rude, and K. Kirkpatrick. 2007. "An Examination of Self-Compassion in Relation to Positive

Psychological Functioning and Personality Traits." *Journal of Research in Personality* 41: 908–916.

Oliver, J. 2011. *The Unwelcome Party Guest—An Acceptance and Commitment Therapy (ACT) Metaphor.* Video. January 31. Retrieved from https://ww w.youtube.com/watch?v=VYht-guymF4.

Pinto–Gouveia, J., C. Duarte, M. Matos, and S. Fráguas. 2014. "The Protective Role of Self–Compassion in Relation to Psycho pathology Symptoms and Quality of Life in Chronic and in Cancer Patients." *Clinical Psychology and Psychotherapy* 21 (4): 311–323.

Porges, S.W. 2007. "The Polyvagal Perspective." *Biological Psychology* 74 (2): 116–143.

Ramnero, J., and N. Törneke. 2008. *The ABCs of Human Behavior: Behavioral Principles for the Practicing Clinician.* Oakland, CA: New Harbinger.

Rockwood, K. 2017. "Frailty and Cardiovascular Care." Presentation at the 27th Annual Cardiovascular Symposium, Current Perspectives in Cardiovascular Disease, Saint John, New Brunswick, September 21–23.

Rod, N.H., M. Kumari, T. Lange, M. Kivimäki, M. Shipley, and J. Ferrie. 2014. "The Joint Effect of Sleep Duration and Disturbed Sleep on Cause-Specific Mortality: Results from the Whitehall II Cohort Study." *PLoS ONE* 9 (4): e91965.

Rosenbaum, M., and R.L. Leibel. 2010. "Adaptive Thermogenesis in Humans." *International Journal of Obesity (London)* 34 (Suppl. 1): S47–S55.

Schmidt, J.B., N.T. Gregersen, S.D. Pedersen, J.L. Arentoft, C. Ritz, T.W. Schwartz, J.J. Holst, A. Astrup, and A. Sjödin. 2014. "Effects of PYY3–36 and GLP-1 on Energy Intake, Energy Expenditure, and Appetite In Overweight Men." *American Journal of Physiology: Endocrinology and Metabolism* 306 (11): E1248–E1256.

Schnall, S., K.D. Harber, J.K. Stefanucci, and D.R. Proffitt. 2008. "Social Support and the Perception of Geographical Slant." *Journal of Experimental Social Psychology* 44 (5): 1246–1255.

Sharma, A. 2017. "Why Redefine Obesity?" Dr. Sharma's Obesity Notes (blog). May 26. http://www.drsharma. ca/why-redefine-obesity.

Siegel, D.J. 2012. *The Developing Mind: How Relationships and the Brain Interact to Shape Who We Are.* 2nd ed. New York: Guilford Press.

Tirch, D.D., B. Schoendorff, and L.R. Silberstein. 2014. *The ACT Practitioner's Guide to the Science of Compassion: Tools for Fostering Psychological Flexibility.* Oakland, CA: New Harbinger.

Tirch, D., L. Silberstein, and R. Kolts. 2018. "Exploring a Process-Focused Approach to Understanding and Practicing Compassion Focused Therapy." Workshop presentation at the Association for Contextual Behavioral

Science World Conference 16, Montreal, Quebec, July 24–29, 2018.

Tremblay, A., M.M. Royer, J.P. Chaput, and E. Doucet. 2013. "Adaptive Thermogenesis Can Make a Difference in the Ability of Obese Individuals to Lose Body Weight." *International Journal of Obesity (London)* 37 (6): 759–764.

Vallis, M. 2015. "Are Behavioural Interventions Doomed to Fail? Challenges to Self-Management Support in Chronic Diseases." *Canadian Journal of Diabetes* 39 (4): 330–334.

Van Pelt, D.W., L.M. Guth, and J.F. Horowitz. 2017. "Aerobic Exercise Elevates Markers of Angiogenesis and Macrophage IL-6 Gene Expression in the Subcutaneous Adipose Tissue of Overweight-to-Obese Adults." *Journal of Applied Physiology* 123 (5): 1150–1159.

Wegner, D.M., D.J. Schneider, S.R. Carter III, and T.L. White. 1987. "Paradoxical Effects of Thought

Suppression." *Journal of Personality and Social Psychology* 53 (1): 5–13.

White, T. 2014. "Most Physicians Would Forgo Aggressive Treatment for Themselves at the End of Life, Study Finds." Stanford Medicine. May 28. http://med.stanford.edu/news/all-news/2014/05/most-physicianswould-forgo-aggressive-treatment-for-themselves-.html. World Health Organization. 2018a. "Diabetes." October 30. http://www.who.int/mediacentre/factsheets/fs312/en.

World Health Organization. 2018b. "Obesity and Overweight." February 16. http://www.who.int/en/news-room/fact-sheets/detail/obesity-and-overweight.

Zessin, U., O. Dickhäuser, and S. Garbade. 2015. "The Relationship Between Self-Compassion and Well-Being: A Meta-Analysis." *Applied Psychology: Health and Well-Being* 7 (3): 340–364.

Zhang, J.W., and S. Chen. 2016. "Self-Compassion Promotes Personal Improvement from Regret Experiences via Acceptance." *Personality and Social Psychology Bulletin* 42 (2): 244–258.

Dayna Lee-Baggley, PhD, exercises regularly and rarely enjoys it. She is a regular runner who competes in 10K races and never gets a runner's high. She drinks green smoothies and hates vegetables. Every time her kid asks her to go do some physical activity (biking, swimming, etc.) she thinks "crap, I don't want to do that," and she does it anyway.

Dayna is also a registered clinical psychologist who specializes in health. She holds an assistant professor appointment in the department of family medicine, and cross appointments in the departments of surgery, and psychology and neuroscience at Dalhousie University; and an adjunct professor appointment in the department of industrial and organizational psychology at Saint Mary's University. She works as a clinical health psychologist at the Nova Scotia Health Authority for the multi-organ transplant program. She is director of the Centre for Behaviour Change, which conducts research and training in chronic disease management. She is an internationally recognized trainer in acceptance and commitment therapy (ACT). She is president of the Atlantic chapter of the Association for Contextual Behavioral Science (ACBS), and vice chair of the Halifax Chapter of the Canadian Obesity Network. She was the recipient of the 2017 Women of Excellence Award for her contributions to health, sport, and wellness (Canadian Progress Club Halifax Cornwallis). Her areas of expertise include facilitating health behavior change, managing and treating obesity, adapting to chronic health conditions, professional resiliency/burnout prevention in health care providers, and healthy workplaces.

Foreword writer **Russ Harris** is an internationally acclaimed ACT trainer, and author of the best-selling ACT-based self-help book, *The Happiness Trap,* which has sold over 600,000 copies and been published in thirty languages. He is widely renowned for his ability to teach ACT in a way that is simple, clear, and fun—yet extremely practical.

MORE BOOKS *from*
NEW HARBINGER PUBLICATIONS

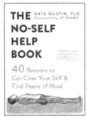

Register your **new harbinger** titles for additional benefits!

When you register your **new harbinger** title—purchased in any format, from any source—you get access to benefits like the following:

- Downloadable accessories like printable worksheets and extra content

- Instructional videos and audio files

- Information about updates, corrections, and new editions

Not every title has accessories, but we're adding new material all the time.

Access free accessories in 3 easy steps:

1. Sign in at NewHarbinger.com (or **register** to create an account).

2. Click on **register a book**. Search for your title and click the **register** button when it appears.

3. Click on the **book cover or title** to go to its details page. Click on **accessories** to view and access files.

That's all there is to it!

If you need help, visit:

NewHarbinger.com/accessories

new harbinger
CELEBRATING
40 YEARS

Back Cover Material

We get it, **being healthy is hard**—here's how to do it anyway

Do you wake up early every morning eager for a run? Do you consider sweet potatoes a splurge? Do you set aside thirty minutes to meditate before work? If so, this book isn't for you. But if you're someone who *thinks* about running and instead falls back to sleep, regrets last night's pizza binge, and can barely get to work on time—let alone meditate beforehand—this in-your-face guide will help you live a healthier life, even if you don't really want to.

In *Healthy Habits Suck,* you *won't* find advice on how to "enjoy" exercise, or tips for making kale taste like chocolate ice cream. What you *will* find are skills to help you actually do the healthy things you know you should be doing. Using the proven-effective techniques in this book, you'll learn to be more mindful about your choices, develop self-compassion, and live a life that reflects what truly matters to you.

Finally, you'll find the motivation you're really craving to adopt healthy habits, even if they do suck.

"A breath of fresh air..."—JASON LILLIS, PhD, COAUTHOR OF THE *DIET TRAP*

"This is one of the most useful and important books I have read for some time." —PAUL FLAXMAN, PHD, COAUTHOR OF *THE MINDFUL AND EFFECTIVE EMPLOYEE*

DAYNA LEE-BAGGLEY, PHD, exercises regularly and rarely enjoys it, and is a runner who never gets a runner's high. She's also a registered clinical psychologist who specializes in helping people to be healthier.

CPSIA information can be obtained
at www.ICGtesting.com
Printed in the USA
BVHW041125070821
613846BV00005B/638